W9-ASC-706

"PAT WIDMER IS TO DOGS WHAT JULIA CHILD IS TO FOOD . . . HER BOOK WILL EQUIP YOU WITH THE KNOWLEDGE OF HOW TO CREATE AN IDEAL PET!"

—*Colorado Humane Society Newsletter*

"Casey, the young dog we found in the mountains of Utah, had never been on a lead, or in a house, or on a sidewalk. Fortunately, we found Pat Widmer in New York City. Pat taught us not only how to train our dog but also that our dog was a unique responsibility we must fulfill. She taught common sense and dog sense as well. She has a lot to say to dog owners and to anyone who is thinking of becoming a dog owner."

—Robert Redford, actor and environmentalist, and Lola Redford, environmentalist and Executive Director, Consumer Action Now

"All the basics of obedience training . . . particularly helpful chapters dealing with specific behavioral problems . . . it has been a valued guide!"

—Gretchen Scanlan, Director, Kent Animal Shelter, Inc.

"Pat Widmer's experience with dogs and, more importantly, her love for these animals has provided the basis of her methods. An obedient dog will be a happy dog if the obedience is taught with sensitivity, affection and firmness. If you follow Pat Widmer, you will achieve that objective."

—Duncan Wright, Executive Director, A.S.P.C.A

PAT WIDMER'S DOG TRAINING BOOK

SIGNET Books of Special Interest

PAT WIDMER'S DOG TRAINING BOOK

STRAIGHT TALK FOR CITY AND SUBURBAN DOG OWNERS

PATRICIA P. WIDMER

Photos by Larry Kalstone

A SIGNET BOOK

NEW AMERICAN LIBRARY

TIMES MIRROR

For Badgerton Dolly and
Julian Augustus, Ber. & Am. C.D.

Contents

Foreword

The kingdom of animals is populated by thousands of different creatures, each with a purpose and a place in nature's backdrop. Most of these creatures hold a fascination for man, and all contribute to his environment. But none has the capacity of a dog for providing companionship and affection.

Most dogs are born into this world relatively unfettered and adaptable to the character and whim of their owner. When one sees a dog that hasn't reached its potential as a companion to man, it is most frequently due to the lack of understanding of the animal by its master.

A myriad of books expressing in various forms the essence of this relationship and how it can be molded have been published, but none that we have read has so succinctly brought into focus the techniques that an owner should use in optimizing his relationship with his dog. It is never necessary to abuse a dog to bring it to the point where it obeys a command or knows its bounds. Pat Widmer's experience with dogs and, more importantly, her love for these animals has provided the basis for her training methods. An obedient dog will be a happy dog if the obedience is taught with sensitivity, affection, and firmness. If you follow the guidelines defined herein, you will achieve that objective.

The result will be a shared affection typifying in all respects the essence of a companion dog and its master.

DUNCAN WRIGHT
Executive Director
*American Society for the Prevention
 of Cruelty to Animals*

Preface

Over the years, how often I have heard clients say, "I don't care about obedience or diet. I just want him housebroken!"

And how often I have then explained that the dog—like the human—is a *total* being, to be looked at and treated in his entirety; that if you deal only with one facet by mechanical means, you simply push the problem into another area. The dog may indeed become housebroken that way. But if the owner is not responding appropriately to the dog's overall needs, the dog may soon become a barker, a chewer, or whatever, albeit a *housebroken* one.

For the sake of your dog's overall needs, I ask you to start at the beginning of this book and read methodically to the end, rather than rushing to the chapter you *believe* fits your situation. The sequence in which I present the information is the result of many years' experience with thousands of clients. This is the sequence in which *you* need the data, the sequence in which success is assured if you will follow the instructions.

Since this book presents a truly overall approach (a method so to speak, rather than a collection of fashionable stopgap procedures), it does not offer advice that can become irrelevant or outdated. The dog will remain a dog; the cat, a cat; and the owner, oh, so human!

PAT WIDMER
New York, 1977

PAT WIDMER'S
DOG TRAINING BOOK

1
Man's Reflection— His Dog

AN APPROACH TO TRAINING

If you sometimes wonder who's running the house, you or your dog, you may be interested in an ancient teaching. According to this bit of wisdom, the domestic animal is a divine gift to man, to provide him his own reflection.

When you acquired your pet, you undoubtedly expected him to mirror a happy, loving home, where affection would be even greater with the presence of a pet. Like many people, you got a dog to improve the quality of your life—to be a companion, amuse the kids, protect the house. How wonderful that new puppy was. Even his *bad* habits were cute. And of course, everyone assumed he would outgrow them anyway. Everyone else's dog did (as far as you knew).

But then things got out of hand. Your friends have begun to say you're crazy to keep the dog. And you've begun to wonder whether you have failed or the dog is mentally defective. Deep in your heart, though, you sense nothing is wrong with the dog. He is a perfectly stable Libra. But what about you?

Yes, as you now realize, your dog is indeed more a reflection of your own state of being than is any other single aspect of your life—including your children, your home, the books in your library, your Gucci loafers, or even your Zodiac ring. His discipline starts and ends with you. Your dog can never be any *better* than you are. He is totally dependent upon your love, your self-discipline, your awareness, your pride.

Your dog's instincts are all correct to begin with; as a puppy he is born intellectually perfect; humans then make him what he is! Whether you train him or ignore him, he lives in your world and *will learn one way or another from the time he is six weeks old. If you set the standards appropriately, he will learn correctly. If you set unsuitable standards (or no standards), he will learn accordingly.*

Before you can expect any change in your dog, you must educate yourself; you must change a little or a lot. Start by thinking of your dog's needs and instincts. He can change only in terms of his own nature, which he had to start with.

There are no impossible dogs, but there are many impossible owners—people who *won't* (not *can't*) grow. If you are one, please do your dog a favor: find him another home *now* before you have made him feel like a complete failure. (The right owner can make any dog the right dog, so find someone who really wants your pet, and send a copy of this book along in his bag.)

If you are willing to change, read on.

Although we all hate to admit it, we really do think of our dogs as little people in fur coats. Indeed, philosophy tells us that a dog is a divine soul in a limited body, just as an infant is a divine soul in a fragile body.

They are certainly little people. In fact, the average dog has the mentality of a 3- to 4-year-old child. But he is also a *dog*, whose canine needs must be met. We must remember this in all we do for our dogs and all we require them to do for us.

As we proceed, you will find that your dog's needs and yours actually coincide as long as you always take care to remember whose needs are being discussed.

Your dog presents you with a unique opportunity to get to know yourself better and perhaps even make some constructive changes. Keep in mind that since the dog's needs and yours really do correspond, a poorly behaved dog (one who presents a problem to you) is also an unhappy dog. Correcting the problem will make both of you happy.

CANINE NEEDS (INSTINCTS)

In order to fulfill our dogs' needs and thereby solve behavioral problems, we must focus on a few principal canine instincts. In doing so, it is particularly important not to project our human neuroses.

The Pack Animal First and most important is consideration of Superdog's instincts as a pack animal. In nature, the dog is a pack animal, living under the dominance of a pack leader whose permission is required in order for an individual dog to do anything.

The pack leader always dominates. He establishes structure and discipline, maintains an orderly, cohesive society. His dominance is often simply through a tone he sets, but he must be ready to defend it when challenged.

You have chosen to take the role that must include being pack leader in your dog's life. You must provide the structure, make the decisions (with consistency, please), enforce them (with fairness, please), and punish misbehavior. Obedience work is not an end in itself, as many think. Rather it's a means of communication (after all, you can't growl well), the means by which you may achieve the status of pack leader and maintain it with the passing of years, at the same time using the obedience training to protect your dog and serve your convenience.

The philosophy involved in obedience training is much like that in being a wise parent whose children both love and *respect* him. NEVER GIVE A COMMAND YOU DO NOT MEAN OR CANNOT ENFORCE! Your dog must know that you will drop whatever you are doing and make him do whatever command you have given. Otherwise, don't give the command. An unenforced command actually teaches disobedience and disrespect.

The Den-Dweller As humans earn more money, have families, and grow older, we tend to think of more space:

larger apartments, grander houses, weekend cottages, ski lodges, and so on. In our minds, space is often related to freedom (from what? . . .). Then we turn around and project the same attitudes toward our dogs. To their detriment.

Not only do we project these human concepts, but we city dwellers also add considerable guilt—guilt that we keep animals "cooped up"—and we thereby make matters even worse. Actually, with strict leash laws, fences, close neighbors, the general disappearance of "space," the suburban dog and the city dog live much the same life. The city dog may not have much of a yard to run in, but he's generally closer to his owner and more people-oriented. Guilt has no place in any relationship between human and dog, so drop it and get on to dealing with your dog's *real* needs.

In his natural state, the dog (like the cat, and like man himself) is a den-dwelling animal. He hunts for food in open areas, plays with his fellow pack members on the plains, urinates and defecates outside the pack's area, but always returns to sleep in a tiny sleeping burrow of his own. This den is often a small hollowed-out space so minute he must turn and turn, making himself seem smaller and smaller, to fit into it. But once there, he feels comfortable, protected, secure. He will never soil his own den, and it is for this reason that we can "housebreak" cats and dogs (the den-dwellers) unlike birds, rabbits, snakes (the non-den-dwellers).

When we want to housebreak a new dog, it is this well-ordered den-dwelling instinct to which we must reach back. We use the dog's own basic instincts for our advantage as well as his pleasure. You will therefore often read in this book of the necessity of providing your dog an adequate den (*tiny* bathroom, kitchen, utility room), *the smaller, the better*, for the times when he is alone in the house. Remember, we're talking about *his* needs, not your human projection of his needs.

Clients often tell me of a dog they know who doesn't need to be left in a den. We all know these dogs—those whose instincts are so strong that they find or make their own dens in whatever space, and those whose instincts are so weak that they have little sense of den. These are perhaps the lucky ones; usually they are spayed bitches, the homebodies of nature. But most dogs evidently do not have such extremes of instinct, and unneutered males certainly have the greatest need for a small den. So don't compare your dog with others. His behavior has already indicated the degree of his need for a den. Just meet his needs.

It is most important, however, that you never confine your dog simply as punishment. In fact, *please give your dog a small food reward every time you put him in his den during the first few weeks of training to make sure neither of you sees it as punishment*. Nor should you put him into his den or any other room in order to avoid having him around when you entertain. Use your obedience training and collar and lead, if necessary, to keep him under control, and *keep him with you*.

Putting him "out of the way" is a rejection mechanism, for which you will pay dearly. Many owners report that by the third or fourth time they attempt to "pitch" the dog out of the way, he bites as they grab for him. Think about it. Stop alienating your dog. Don't create confrontations.

Also, your dog must sleep in a room with a human being at night. He may sleep in his own bed (not wicker, please; it splinters if he chews it), on a blanket on the floor, on your bed, wherever you wish. But in the room with you. Putting him elsewhere will generally result in your being greeted with a pile of shit first thing in the morning—or worse yet, a mass of floor tiles ripped up during the night. Putting him out of the bedroom at night constitutes an extreme form of rejection and robs him of one of the pleasantest times he can spend with you with no effort on your part.

These Instincts May Have Been Suppressed If you start training with a young puppy, you will have relatively few problems assuming the role of pack leader or "denning" him. Those pure instincts reinforced by his dam (mother) will be fresh in his mind, and the most you will get is a little backtalk—just like a fresh kid trying out his new vocabulary. But if you are working out things with a dog over six months of age (not old by any means; in fact, they're never too old as long as they can move) you may actually have *suppressed* his natural instincts for so long that you will have to work to get back to them. You can do so and can do it within a few days, but it will mean that you must be totally determined when you establish his den—putting him in it with a sense of absolute necessity (never for punishment, please)—and when you become pack leader via the obedience work.

Know that those instincts are indeed there. There is no such animal as a dog lacking pack or den instinct. But recall that *you* have buried them deeply by your own behavior, so you must work at getting back to them.

EYE CONTACT

Since you must learn to be a good and fair pack leader as part of solving your dog's problems, you must also understand the workings of eye contact and begin to see how it functions in dealing with your dog. First, recall the "stare down" games of your childhood. Or consider how nervous you become when a strange person on a bus sits and stares, and stares.

Eye contact is part of you dog's world, perhaps a very important part. A "strong-eye" is considered a necessity in a good herding dog, for it is this "strong eye" that holds the sheep or cattle. Most dogs, in fact, show great awareness of eye contact. When two unacquainted dogs approach one another, they make eye contact first, from a distance. Often, one drops his gaze and they continue on. In other cases, both dogs drop to the ground, eyes fixed upon one another, until some magic tells them which is superior, which inferior, and they continue. Or if they are equal and both males, there may well be a fight if their owners do not restrain them.

A puppy who makes eye contact with an approaching adult dog or human, will roll over on its back, urinate a bit, perhaps show a "smile"—all signs set off by the eye contact and intended to indicate submission. Bitches (female dogs) often do the same with males and with humans upon initial meeting. Since this eye contact can set off fights between dogs, provoke aggression directed at a person by a dog, and cause "submissive urination" and many other incidents, it behooves the dog owner to keep this natural reaction in mind. It will be referred to later and must be dealt with appropriately in a number of problem-solving situations.

THE STATE OF YOUR MIND WHEN YOU PICK UP THAT LEAD

When you approach training, you will often be tempted to slough off instructions by saying, "Ah, he doesn't really want to . . . " Think for a moment: "Whose desires am I talking about, his or mine?" At the same time, rid your mind of all those tales of traumas your dog has suffered that "explain" his idiosyncrasies. Those of us who train dogs professionally get weary of these "excuses." No, the fact that he arrived by air on a very turbulent flight from Iowa at six weeks of age does *not* account for his biting your sister-in-law five years later. But you might just consider his puppy-mill breeding, his not being neutered at six months of age, a total lack of structure and discipline, and maybe even the fact that you loathe your sister-in-law—and get to work rectifying these situations.

Have three things straight in your own mind before training your dog.

You must: 1) want to train, 2) communicate pleasure to your dog, and 3) take pleasure in his performance. How can you expect him to enjoy it if you don't? If he doesn't wag his tail when you praise him, look to your own tone of voice, your mood.

Don't train when you don't feel like it. On the other hand, when you're under stress, you'll find working with your dog the greatest therapy. It gives you the perfect opportunity to turn your attention away from yourself and your problems and onto the dog. This turning of the attention outward is always necessary in training, but particularly helpful during periods of stress in the owner's life. You both benefit.

AUTHORITY LEVEL

And speaking of attitude, tone of voice, and the reaction to it, have you ever noticed how most dogs seem to obey men better than women and that men seem to have fewer problems with their dogs? For those of you who have read the feminist literature, there will be no difficulty understanding this phenomenon. But for the rest of you, let me explain, since this point is crucial to training.

Generations of women were not brought up to be authoritative, to demand, to declare their beliefs in plain, straightforward language. Unlike men, women were supposed to be "gentle," discreet, even devious; certainly not direct, and most definitely they were not to be leaders in the public eye. But these are the very qualities the dog requires of you and responds to, the qualities of a pack leader. He wants to know, in the simplest, most direct, authoritative terms possible. He prefers, "Heel, dammit!" to, "Heel, god willing . . . ?"

In order for women and children to train their dogs effectively, they must adopt pack-leader characteristics, maintain them, and—harder yet—carry them out in public: on the streets, in stores, and in their own homes in front of guests. Yes, onlookers will be appalled. Yes, they will interfere. They will kibitz; they may even threaten. This is perfectly normal. After all, the world hasn't changed yet. Male Chauvinist Pig isn't a term of the past.

Do you recall the time you disciplined a whining child on the bus? All those glares you got? Well, here you go again, this time with a dog. Don't be intimidated. You do indeed know what you're doing, and a very few weeks from now, when your dog is behaving beautifully, the same people who criticize today will—with great respect—ask how you did it. You can tell them you began by working on your own authority level—then the dog.

While we're on the subject of chauvinism, you feminists may be interested to learn that although women have greater problems projecting the required amount of authority with dogs, female dogs exhibit fewer behavioral problems of any type. Throughout many years of professional training. I have found that only about ten percent of our clients have encountered difficulties of sufficient severity to require outside assistance to train bitches.

From here on in this book, dogs are generally referred to as male, since most people in need of this book will have male dogs (and will vow to have a bitch next time!). And many of the serious readers will be women, because women, single or married, seem much more likely to sense the need for training help. The single man, alone with his problem dog, usually seems to decide the *dog* is impossible and therefore gets rid of him; perhaps on occasion he just suffers in silence. He isn't likely to call a professional trainer.

THE DOG HIMSELF

We all hear about the differences in the trainability of various breeds. Yet every trainer must train all breeds, and all breeds do indeed get trained. So we must conclude the differences among the breeds offer no major deterrent other than to require a little more or less effort, a little more or less time. What is significant, however, is the difference in the *owners* of different breeds. Obviously, people choose a breed, or mixed breed for that matter, with an image in mind. This image then predisposes the owner. For example, few Afghan owners bother to train because they expect their dogs to be "beautiful but dumb." Owners of German Shepherd Dogs on the other hand, frequently train their pets because they expect another Rin Tin Tin. And Shetland Sheepdogs (what many call "miniature collies") must have become top-rated obedience dogs because their owners just *know* they are working dogs, and few of us keep sheep! So if you are carrying around any negative images, drop them before you start training. You will be amazed how fast your dog smartens up!

Intelligence is not the only quality about which we have all sorts of misconceptions. How about size? We tend to think it *must* be easier to live with a Toy Poodle than a Great Dane. And we acquire our Poodle with that thought firmly in mind. Well, I'll grant you it's hard to coexist with a Dane bent on destruction. But simply because of the Dane's size, his owner is usually more aware of his dog's behavior and tends to take action on a problem more quickly than will the Poodle's. After all, how much harm can an "itsy bitsy" do when he bites or urinates on the carpet? Quite a bit! So if you have just got your small dog, make up your mind that you surely do have a dog—not *half* a dog.

B. F. SKINNER WOULD APPROVE

All the training methods presented here are based on behavior modification by positive reinforcement. You set up an environment in which things cannot go wrong, motivate the dog to pleasing, instinctive behavior, and reward him for it with praise and love. Somehow we must keep in mind that dogs, like people, should be loved and respected, as well as rewarded, for good behavior. We have to become as discriminating with our dogs as with people. We must respond to character and behavior rather than looks and charm.

The terms "training" "discipline," and "structure" do not in any way imply less love and affection for your pet. They simply describe canine needs in addition to love, play, and affection. I don't object to your dog's sleeping on the bed or sitting in your lap watching television if that's your choice. But loved dogs and spoiled dogs are two different things. The loved dog lives in an atmosphere of sufficient structure and is a very secure animal. The spoiled dog (he who exercises his "right" to do whatever he wants whenever he wants even if it is extremely annoying to the owner) quickly becomes neurotic, even psychotic, extremely unhappy, and eventually a terrible burden to his owner and himself.

So you must remind yourself from time to time that Superdog *is a dog*. He can never be otherwise. There is no miracle that will make him into a child or eliminate his canine instincts. Your dog is an individual being with needs of his own. He demands respect even more than love, and he has an occasional desire for privacy. He cannot be absorbed into your personality. Nor can he replace a child or lover. He can, however, offer love, warmth, respect, companionship, protection. These characteristics all in one being should be enough for anyone!

I cannot stress too often or too strongly that all instructions must be followed to the letter. Otherwise, you will not fulfill all your dog's needs; he will tell you so by poor behavior. Dogs are very predictable. If you set up a disaster, you'd better believe he'll fall into it. Six weeks after you start training, you shouldn't be able to remember the last time you had occasion to punish your dog; if you can, you aren't doing your job!

By the way, one of my clients advises that *reading* this book to your dog will serve no purpose. She tried it for half an hour each day with no result whatsoever other than improving her own reading speed and voice quality.

2

It All Starts in the Veterinarian's Office

YOUR DOG'S HEALTH AS IT RELATES TO TRAINING

Your dog's health should be a matter of great concern to you. But what you may not have considered is that his health also is relevant to training. Many behavioral problems originate with or are aggravated by poor health.

Therefore, try to choose a competent (ask your dog-owning friends) veterinarian *before* you acquire your puppy, and take the puppy to him immediately for a checkup. (Don't hesitate to return the puppy if he so advises. An unhealthy puppy can cost you more money and cause you more anguish than you would believe, and your keeping him will actually encourage the seller to continue his poor treatment of animals.)

You will learn that puppies are given temporary immunization shots before the age of twelve weeks and a "permanent" Distemper-Hepatitis-Leptospirosis inoculation at twelve weeks. It shouldn't really be called "permanent," because it must be repeated each year on the anniversary of the first one. The dog should be inoculated against Rabies by six months of age if not earlier, and again, a booster is given periodically, the frequency depending upon the type of vaccine. Your veterinarian will advise you. In any event, the puppy may *not* be walked outside or come into contact with other dogs before receiving the "permanent" Distemper-Hepatitis-Leptospirosis shot at twelve weeks of age.

You will also find that many puppies have worms. Worms give puppies diarrhea, make them urinate and defecate erratically, create a need to chew, and generally make them edgy and irritable. Dogs bought from pet shops especially have frequent recurrences of worm infestation. Often, worms are likely to have been present in the puppy at birth, having been transmitted by his mother.

The most common way in which dogs become worm-infested beyond puppyhood is by stepping in the feces of worm-infested dogs. These feces contain the worm eggs, which are ingested when the dog licks (cleans) his feet.

Now, here's a point to zero in on: worm eggs in feces cannot survive long on pavement, but they do live and multiply in soil. Got that? So if you live in a city, be sure you housebreak your own dog to the street and avoid walking him in any soil area that other dogs have used to defecate in. If you live in a house, don't let a worm-infested dog (yours or anyone else's) defecate on your property, or you may end up with a dog who re-infests every few weeks. And that's a nightmare!

Every few weeks on puppies, and at least once a year on mature dogs, have a fecal sample checked by your veterinarian. And do it again whenever you suspect a behavioral problem may be caused by worm infestation.

The fecal sample check may reveal round worm, hook worm, or whip worm. Tapeworm may be diagnosed if you see grains resembling rice in the dog's stool.

Heartworm is a whole different thing. These large worms lodge in the right side of the dog's heart, interfering with its function. You may suspect heart worm infestation if your dog becomes tired easily, gasps for breath, or coughs. However, when you notice these symptoms, the infestation has reached major proportions.

It is more to the point to have your dog tested annually with a simple blood test. Since heartworm is carried by mosquitos from one infected dog to another, your dog obviously can contract it only during the mosquito months.

Your veterinarian may very well wish to put your dog on a preventive medication during that part of the year. But whether your dog takes a preventive or not, he should be given a blood test to check for heartworm annually, six to eight months after the end of the mosquito season where you live.

If it is necessary for you to give your dog the heartworm preventive in pill form (or to give him any other medication in tablet or capsule), you will find it easy to do if you imbed the medication in a *small* piece of soft cheese, liverwurst, margarine, or other particularly appetizing substance. Be sure the piece is small enough just to cover the medication. If it's large, the dog will chew it, find the pill in the middle, spit out what he doesn't like, and eat only the goodie.

A word of advice on how to prevent your dog from catching some of the more common dog illnesses.

First of all, never take your dog into a pet shop that sells dogs. Shops that offer only supplies and grooming should be safe. But every germ in the world is apt to be walking around the pet shop that sells dogs. So avoid them at all costs. If you go into such a shop, *never* take your dog in with you.

Second, don't let your dog socialize with dogs unknown to you, particularly unkempt dogs. Chances are they don't see a veterinarian any more often than they see a groomer. Be a snobbish owner!

Other health concerns develop with the dog. For instance, the male dog's testicles usually descend by the time he is four to five months of age, six months at the latest. Dogs with one or no testicles (cryptorchids, as they are called) may not be exhibited in the breed classes at dog shows, nor should they ever be bred. Most are sterile. However, veterinarians believe such dogs should be neutered in order to prevent the development of tumors around the undescended testicle. Be sure to consult your veterinarian if your dog's testicles do not descend normally.

If you have a bitch (female dog), you may expect her to come into season any time from six months of age (five months in toy breeds). Before her season, she may urinate frequently and uncontrollably. This behavior is normal before the season, but at any other time it indicates a serious health problem.

Many dogs who have been in pet shop cages for long periods have housebreaking—that is, frequent urination—difficulties because constant caging, requiring them to urinate and defecate in their own den, represses the dog's natural instincts of cleanliness. If you have a pet shop dog with frequent urination problems, however, it is advisable to have a test done to see whether he is capable of concentrating his urine before you assume his difficulties are the result of long caging.

Stool-eating (coprophagy) does not generally reflect a health irregularity. The vast majority of dogs, if left with their own feces or another animal's, will sooner or later eat them. All kinds of remedies have been suggested over the years. I haven't seen any success except by cleaning up *before* the dog can get to it. And stop regarding your dog's stool-eating as some sort of perversion. It's perfectly normal!

I hardly need to tell you that young puppies have very tiny, needle-sharp teeth. But you will be relieved to learn that they lose all those puppy teeth between the ages of four months and six months, replacing them with heavier, less sharp, adult teeth. If your pet has any puppy teeth left by seven months (or earlier if you neuter him or her prior to that age), those teeth should be removed by the veterinarian so that they do not cause continued discomfort and further gnawing at anything and everything.

The dog's teething period is similar to a child's. It may go easily, with few noticeable signs. Or it may go hard, with diarrhea, poor eating, unscheduled urinating, running eyes, and so on. Your dog is particularly vulnerable during this period, so don't expose him to drafts or sick dogs. Keep him supplied with chewies and ice cubes. And for those especially difficult days, put a wet, twisted wash cloth in the freezer and give it to him frozen to numb his gums as he chews on it. He may have baby aspirin (flavored) three times a day, but the quantity depends upon his body weight. Check with your veterinarian for the proper dosage.

Don't leave a teething dog alone, out of sight, for one second during this period. Don't tie him at night near anything he can chew. And don't leave him loose in your bedroom while you sleep unless you want to awaken to a reasonable facsimile of a Salvation Army furniture depot. Above all, watch those electric cords! And throughout the teething period if it's a tough one, keep reminding yourself that at least puppies grow up faster than children.

If you notice your dog shaking his head or rubbing it on furniture or rugs a good deal, he is most likely having difficulties with his ears, eyes, or teeth. Take him to a veterinarian promptly before you have a major illness on your hands.

Bad breath in your dog is most likely to be caused by poor diet, tartar on teeth, or decayed teeth. Occasionally it results from more serious health problems and is certainly not to be ignored or covered up. Excessive tartar buildup and tooth decay are best prevented by feeding your dog a kibble diet. Dry kibble gives the dog something to chew, which keeps his teeth and gums clean and healthy.

Ticks and fleas are a genuine health concern as well as an annoyance. They will annoy your dog, infest your home, and eventually harass you. Fleas are small oblong black bugs, just big enough to see. They jump quickly from spot to spot. You most often see them in the lighter hair on the dog's stomach. They may be treated with a special flea bath. You can buy the shampoo in a pet shop. Follow instructions on the bottle, and also get some flea powder to put in the dog's bed to kill any fleas there. You might consider putting a flea medallion (better than the flea collar) on his regular collar. But remember to change it at required intervals, and do follow all directions on the box.

If you continually have flea problems, talk to your veterinarian about tapeworm. Generally, where you find fleas, you find tapeworm since the flea is the intermediate host to one form of tapeworm. Your dog may pick up this tapeworm if he eats fleas containing tapeworm eggs.

Ticks are an even greater problem. They are small round bugs, either brown or black, with legs you can see. They generally fasten themselves firmly into the dog's skin. Remove them with tweezers. Put iodine on the bite immediately. Destroy the ticks by burning them or flushing them down the toilet—you can't kill ticks any other way. If you find more than a few ticks, your dog should be tick-bathed. You can buy tick shampoo at the pet shop or get it from your veterinarian. If you continue to find ticks on the dog after removing them all once, your home should be fumigated. A professional exterminator can do it, or you can buy inexpensive foggers (actually just a type of aerosol can) from your veterinarian and do the job yourself. Just follow the instructions on the can. And then start thinking about where the dog picked up the ticks and stop taking him there. For added insurance, buy him a tick collar. Read the instructions on the box carefully, and follow them. Tick collars contain very strong ingredients, not to be played around with.

Many household accidents befall dogs, as they do us. Your veterinarian should be consulted upon such occasions. But there is one mishap that bears mentioning because it's not the accident itself that harms the dog, but rather the owner's attempt to treat the mishap.

Dogs are curious creatures who always have to be in the middle of everything, particularly when you are painting the house. They end up with a spot of paint on the tail, another along the side, perhaps a green ear, whatever. Then the well-meaning owner tries to "neaten up" Superdog with a little paint remover. Within seconds the dog is howling in pain, leaping around the house as if on fire, knocking over treasures and trash alike.

Paint thinners, paint removers, and other such liquids have a much greater effect on animals than they have on us. They burn fiercely, panicking the animal completely. Better to leave the paint on the dog until it simply wears off. Or if the coat is long and becomes tangled with the paint, cut off some hair. If you must remove paint or tar, however, use salad oil or mineral oil to do so. Better still, keep the dog out of the paint to begin with. But if someone in your house should inadvertently try to remove paint from the dog with a chemical that burns, wash the area with lots of soap and water immediately and call your veterinarian quickly.

Clients of mine often call to ask about a dog's vomiting. It not only worries them but also upsets eating schedules and therefore housebreaking schedules. A dog can regurgitate at will and may freqently do so simply because of a hair in his throat or because he's angry with you. It is reasonably easy to tell whether the dog is really sick or just clearing its throat, so to speak. A healthy dog will vomit and then eat what it has just regurgitated. A dog who doesn't feel well will simply walk away. So leave the mess there long enough to see whether Superdog will do you the favor of cleaning it up himself.

Some dogs spit up small amounts of saliva (white) or bile (yellow) fairly regularly without being ill in any way. Repeated vomiting, however, is cause for concern and should be reported to your veterinarian immediately. En route to the phone, though, pick up any food or water that may be available to the dog and keep them out of reach until your veterinarian advises otherwise.

3

You May Be the French Chef, But . . .

DIET

Diet is so important to your dog's physical condition and behavior that I could not attempt to answer any questions or solve any problems without first making sure you understand every detail of diet and feed your dog properly—right food, right quantity, right time of the day.

First, let's dispose of all those "finicky dog" stories. "Finicky dogs" belong to people with food hangups, with "Jewish mother" complexes. It is normal for a dog to be hungry all the time, to eat anything edible (and sometimes inedible), to eat the same thing every day and love it. If yours doesn't fall into this category, make up your mind that he will immediately.

If your dog doesn't eat anything put in front of him and doesn't always eat all his food, you won't be able to use his appetite as a yardstick for his general health. In other words, if he seems not to like his chicken soufflé Monday, or the veal scallopine Tuesday, or the beef Wellington Wednesday, you won't take him to the veterinarian until Thursday, because you'll figure your cooking isn't up to par. But your veterinarian won't be amused. Because three days after the act, your dog may be pretty sick, so sick in fact that he may not make it. But his chances would have been 100% better if on Monday you had flung a dish of dog food on the floor at

7:00 a.m. and when by 7:30 a.m. he hadn't devoured it a usual, you had called the doctor. Yes, you may be th "French Chef," but you failed as far as your dog i concerned.

So make up your mind right now. You wouldn't permit child to eat nothing but chocolate malteds. You shouldn't le your dog choose his food either—if you want to keep hir around, that is.

All research indicates that dogs should eat *dog food;* it' the best-balanced food available to them. You couldn' duplicate its nutritional value in your own kitchen withou hours and hours of work. Even then, something woul surely be missing.

The ideal form of dog food is the totally dry, crunchy foo that goes by the generic term "Kibble" from the Englis expression "kibbled bisquit." Unfortunately, you won't find that word on the box, so simply look for foods that come ir boxes or large bags and are completely dry and hard. The kibble sold in supermarkets or professional feed dealers is a good balance of protein and other needed nutrients. It is ar excellent diet for the average adult dog and is used as such by most professionals: kennel owners, shelter managers veterinarians, trainers, and groomers. It is easy to store, easy to feed, and the cheapest form of food. The hard chunks wil keep the dog's teeth clean and his gums healthy throughout his life.

Incidentally, if you have a large dog or several dogs or cats, find the name and phone number of a professional feed dealer in your classified phone directory and order kibble, cat food, litter, vitamins, and so on delivered to your home in quantity. Costs will be substantially lower.

Before we explore the uses of kibble and the appropriate ways to feed it to different dogs, I must tell you a few things about the other types of dog food. Canned food has been around for years. There is the canned food that claims to be "all meat." Well, it certainly is "all" something—usually all out of balance. And full of moisture (read the label on the can—something like 75% moisture), an expensive way to buy water. Also, there is canned food containing many different ingredients, including cereal, which is well-balanced. In fact, its content is usually the same as kibble. Except that again it generally contains about 75 to 80% moisture.

And then there are the soft-moist foods, the most recent, addition to the canine menu. These are actually *people-oriented* foods that look like hamburger or chunks of meat. They are laden with sugar, and oh, what they do to housebreaking and to our city streets! These foods are manufactured in such a way that they balloon out in the dog's body, absorbing all the moisture in his system, making him drink lots of water, and creating vast amounts of feces. The result is that the dog urinates and defecates several times the amount he would on any other diet. Disaster! Ruined carpets, filthy streets, and many a dog-training business sprouting overnight to take care of all those "unhousebreakable" dogs.

Also available are special, prescription dog foods in both the canned and soft-moist form. These may be bought only upon prescription from a veterinarian and should be used only for dogs with specific illnesses—kidney disease, heart disease, digestive problems, or weight problems. There is even a prescription diet for puppies under seven weeks of age, being weaned. If you have a dog on one of these diets, make sure your other pets do not share its food. The prescription diets have been purposely *un*balanced in order to suit the sick dog's particular condition.

Over the years many old wives' tales have made the rounds in the field of dog nutrition. For instance, generations of dog lovers have fed their dogs raw eggs "for a glossy coat." Yet, raw eggs contain an enzyme, avidin, that prevents the vitamin biotin from being absorbed by the dog. Protein does help coat condition, as do vitamins A, D, and E. But not *raw eggs*!

Then there's dairy milk. Most puppies get diarrhea from milk, but how often the well-meaning dog owner gives it, until he must cart the dehydrated pup off to the veterinarian, who advises against milk and suggests cottage cheese.

This saga wouldn't be complete without mentioning garlic. "They" used to say that feeding a dog garlic kept it free of worms. Just as "they" used to say wearing garlic around your neck kept you in good health, or free from evil spirits, or whatever. Save the garlic for the soup. Your dog doesn't need it any more than you need it around your neck.

There are, however, additives that will benefit your dog. A coat conditioner is perhaps the most important. It will keep his coat glossy and free of excess dandruff. It should be put into his food daily for his entire life. No, I don't believe cooking oil will do. It seems not to be properly balanced for the dog, and it's more expensive than the basic coat-conditioning dietary additive available by the quart or gallon at pet shops and variety stores.

Also, puppies and older dogs should be given a multiple vitamin daily in liquid, powder, or tablet form. These are available from veterinarians or pet shops. The quality is the same, but the price at the pet shop is considerably lower.

Now for the diet itself. First, let's consider the content, then the quantity and schedule.

Start with a basic diet of kibble, *fed dry* (my veterinarian says, "If it goes in dry, it comes out dry." Pretty good advice, no?). Add coat conditioner (and vitamin for the puppy or older dog). And that's it for the *normal* adult dog.

But what about other dogs?

DIETS FOR OTHER DOGS

The Hyperactive Adult Dog Diet: ⅔ kibble, ⅓ pasta (spaghetti-type food, cooked of course. For your own convenience, make a batch once a week).

The Hyperactive, Skinny Adult Dog Diet: ⅓ kibble, ⅓ pasta; remaining ⅓ a combination of cream cheese (regular form, not low-calorie) and white bread or bagel or something similar; also, add Tiger's Milk™—1 tablespoon a day for a toy dog; 2 tablespoons for a small dog; 3 tablespoons for a medium-size dog; 4 to 6 tablespoons for large breeds.

The Obese Dog Diet: Straight kibble in *minute* quantity; if your dog is not only fat but also extremely inactive, use a very tiny amount of dry kibble and some protein source such as cottage cheese, scrambled egg, or chopped beef (raw). But keep the overall quantity very small—such as 3 level table-spoons of food a day, *total*, for an obese cocker spaniel. Please don't project, as one client did. She tells me she lost weight along with the dog because she wouldn't eat in front of him!

The Puppy Diet: ⅓ kibble, ⅓ cottage cheese, ⅓ additional protein: cooked eggs, raw chopped beef (very low grade, 50% fat). If yours is a very large breed, modify this combination slightly so that the diet is ½ kibble, ¼ cottage cheese, and ¼ other protein source. Otherwise, you won't be able to afford to feed yourself! As the puppy matures, increase the proportion of kibble and decrease the proportion of additional protein so as to arrive at an all-kibble diet by the dog's adulthood.

The Older Dog Diet: As dogs get older, they, like humans, require less protein. In fact, their kidneys cannot cope with large amounts of protein. So, as your dog advances in age, make sure no additional protein whatsoever is provided with the kibble. This means no eggs, no meats, no cheese, no fish, no poultry. The kibble, which contains protein of approxi-mately 19 to 23%, will be quite adequate. Do not use a high-protein kibble, puppy kibble (which is also high in protein), or any other form that indicates protein content in excess of 23%. If possible, use a brand with a lower protein content.

NO BONES,* NO CANDY, NO JUNK FOOD, PLEASE!

How Much Food for Your Dog?: (1) Normal weight, unneutered adult dogs living in a suburban house or city

---

*In addition to heeding the oft-quoted fact that splintered bones can puncture the dog's intestines or stomach, consider a more common problem caused by bone-eating: severe constipation. If Superdog gets hold of a bone that he can chew to bits (and there are few he can't devour), the small bone chips mix with the intestinal contents to form clay-colored, hard, dry stools the consistency of mortar.

apartment generally eat about 1 cup of the appropriate foregoing diet per 15 lb. of body weight.

(2) Obese dogs should eat only about ⅓ of that amount.

(3) Very thin dogs may eat more than dogs of normal weight. But remember: there is no point in feeding a dog any food he can't use. If you find he defecates more than three times a day, you are probably overfeeding. He may indeed be hungry, even thin. But no matter how much you feed him, if his metabolism doesn't use the food, it's just going to go right through him.

(4) Spayed or castrated pets should eat about ½ to ¾ cup per 15 lb. of body weight.

Obviously, dogs living under circumstances that provide great amount of exercise should be fed more. But don't judge by the quantities suggested on the dog-food packages. The manufacturers are selling dog food and couldn't care less if you have to clean up with a snow shovel.

Puppies during growing stages—which are off and on—generally require almost twice as much food as an adult dog. Generally you can feed a puppy all it will eat, unless it is becoming fat or is defecating more than four or five times a day (a sign that the body is not using the food but is just throwing it off).

And what is a puppy and what is a grown or adult dog? Usually the toy breeds are considered puppies until six months of age; the small breeds until seven to eight months; the medium-size breeds until a year; the giant breeds until eighteen months.

The toy dog eats three meals a day at twelve weeks of age; two meals a day from about fourteen weeks to five or six months; thereafter one meal a day.

The small dog follows the same schedule as the toy dog.

The medium-size dog eats three meals a day until he's about five months of age; two meals a day to a year; thereafter one meal a day.

The large and giant breeds eat three meals a day until about seven months of age; thereafter two meals a day. (If you have a large or giant breed, be sure to discuss the subject of bloat with the breeder from whom you get the dog or with your veterinarian.)

Your puppy will generally tell you, by refusing to eat, when he is ready to cut out one meal a day. But don't necessarily drop the meal he refuses. He refuses by chance. You schedule by choice.

When you're feeding three meals a day, schedule them this way: 1) in the morning 2) in midafternoon if you're home (otherwise the minute your return in the evening), and 3) again later in the evening.

When you switch the dog from three meals to two, feed: 1) first thing in the morning, and 2) again *early* in the evening.

When your dog graduates to one meal a day, that meal should be in the morning when you arise so that he starts the day satisfied and has energy available to him over the day. He'll sleep at night when his energy is lowest. Also, since the dog's digestive cycle is approximately twenty-two hours, feeding him in the morning will assure that he defecates regularly and easily every morning. (Obviously, if you work at night and sleep by day, you should feed your dog in the evening when you get up.)

It cannot be overemphasized that *diet is the key to good health and housekeeping*. Don't expect a housebroken dog if you don't feed him properly.

On that subject again, your dog is to eat what is best for him. Period. If you have not been feeding him a basic *dry* kibble diet, he may resist the switch and not eat for a few days. (I have seen one dog hold out for five days, but he has been happily eating his kibble ever since). You must be patient and wait out the resistance. Put his food down on the floor for twenty minutes. Whatever is then left (all of it, perhaps) gets put in the fridge until the next regular meal time. He won't starve himself to death—even to spite his "Jewish mother!"

If you have been feeding your adult dog in the evening, simply skip one day's feeding (how about today's?) and feed him the next morning. No, he won't starve. Don't feed him both his regular evening meal and a meal the next morning. You'll be causing housebreaking problems.

An adult dog should have water with meals and whenever you are home. Puppies should be offered water with meals and as indicated on the housebreaking schedule. Do *not* leave water in your dog's den unless you are following specific instructions to leave his food there also (see chapter on Chewing Problems). In any case, water should be ice cold so that his thirst will be quenched quickly and he'll drink considerably less.

4
Sex and the Single Dog

Remarks of Dr. Michael Fox, associate professor of psychology, Washington University, St. Louis, at the Dog Health Seminar in King of Prussia, Pa. February 4, 1973:

"Wild canids only have one heat period a year and the males only produce sperm during this short breeding season. They reach sexual maturity between 1-2 years of age and are often monogamous. Such aspects of sexual behavior must have been changed early on in domesticating the dog in order to increase productivity. Dogs are mature sexually by 6-8 months, males constantly produce sperm and sexual promiscuity has replaced monogamy. . . . We have essentially made dogs hypersexual and they are ill-adapted for urban life since few dogs are ever satisfied sexually. . . . In view of the obvious frustrations, combined with the enormous problem of too many unwanted puppies, a kindness to help urban dogs adapt would be massive castration and spaying programs. Only licensed breeders should be permitted to have fertile pets."

"A spayed or castrated animal also makes a better pet because it is often less aggressive. Normally when a dog reaches sexual maturity, it engages in status fights. Around 1-2 years of age, a pet dog begins to test its master and other members of the household to see how much social freedom it might have. An over-indulged pet often turns out to be the alpha or number one leader of the household pack.

"This is the genesis of the socially maladjusted canine delinquent! . . . A well-adjusted dog is one that has been dominated psychologically and occasionally physically, early in life, by its master . . . . (and is also loved)."

The sweet voice on the other end of the line proclaimed: "Boris is going to get laid!"

After muttering, "That's interesting," I asked why. My client explained that she loved him so much she thought there should be more Borises around and that also, she felt she should contribute to his sexual education and fulfillment. If you have any of these attitudes, read on.

I explained that she must then be prepared to live in a urinal, since male dogs, once they're bred, usually go around lifting their legs (urinating) all over the house. To boot, they often become more aggressive with dogs and sometimes even with people. I further pointed out that although Boris was a nice kid, he was not "show quality," much less a champion, and that breeding him would do the breed as a whole no good. And if she really loved Boris and Lhasas in general (and she did!), the best thing to do was *not* breed him.

After this conversation, the client at my suggestion made a few calls to noted breeders who confirmed what I'd told her. In addition, they pointed out that no one with a good bitch would permit her to be bred to this poor-quality non-champion. So my client couldn't even get Boris a respectable girl friend! Boris didn't get "laid," and everyone lived happily ever after. Particularly Boris.

For the rest of you dog owners, however, let's go into more detail. Sex for the male dog is a force he must comply with if he's given the opportunity. For him, it's not the pleasure that we humans seem to dwell upon. Sex is simply something that nature compels him to do when he's in the presence of a bitch in season. It will not "satisfy his sexual urges" (a dog's mounting other dogs is a natural energy release or attempt to dominate; his mounting people just indicates he's not getting enough exercise) and in fact will make them considerably worse. He doesn't sit around all day contemplating his next affair, nor does he have any interest in the pups he may sire. Sorry to disillusion you, but that's nature.

As for the bitch, her seasons will begin anytime around six months of age and occur usually twice a year. Each will last in one form or another for as long as four weeks. The time she can be bred generally, but not necessarily, follows the heaviest bleeding. Before she comes into season, she is apt to urinate frequently and may seem to forget her housebreaking. After her season, she may experiece false pregnancies during which she builds a nest, secretes milk in her mammary glands, and actually thinks she will whelp a litter. When she does not, she may become very upset, nervous, and aggressively self-protective.

The answer to false pregnancies, messy heat periods, awkward confinements, and a high likelihood of cancer or pyometra (a very dangerous, often fatal uterine infection) is of course to have her spayed as early as possible—usually at six months of age. She does *not* have to come into season once before being spayed. Spaying frequently also calms a nervous or high-strung bitch.

This operation has been routine for many years, but many people still do not know what it involves. Actually a hysterectomy is performed, under total anesthesia, leaving a very small incision usually closed with three or four stitches that must be removed a week to ten days later. Most private veterinarians prefer to keep the bitch two or three days; many neutering clinics keep them just overnight. In any case, she will come home full of bounce, in no mood to "recuperate." Would that we humans were so fortunate! And no, she won't get fat and lazy when spayed unless you, the dog owner, overfeed her.

And what of the male dog? The unneutered male dog tends to roam (many literally run away) and become uncontrollable in the presence of a bitch in season. With his increased hormone activity at about six months of age and continuing to eighteen months or more, he is prone toward leg-lifting indoors as well as out, hyperactivity, and aggression. These problems are easily prevented by early (before a year of age) neutering, which has become quite common in recent years, particularly since it is required by most humane societies before dogs are adopted.

But you may not know how the neutering is done, and you may appreciate an explanation in layman's terms. The veterinarian anesthetizes the dog completely, makes a small incision in front of the scrotum, removes the testicle, and then stitches the incision closed, usually with three or four stitches. Most veterinarians prefer to keep the dogs overnight. In any case, expect the dog to come home in normal high spirits.

Afterward, the dog will look the same except for the stitches, which must be removed a week or two later. With the passing of time, the scrotum will atrophy and disappear.

Hormonal changes will occur gradually over a period of six to eight weeks. Although neutering will cut down aggression, it will not affect the dog's protective behavior. In fact, protective behavior generally will increase, since dogs protect best when they relate to people well and the neutered dog is much closer to his owner than the unneutered dog. No, he won't get fat and lazy unless *you* overfeed him.

And what of breeding in general? Naturally, the pure breeds can be continued only by breeding. But I'd hope that only the finest dogs will be bred (and then only in limited numbers), not the poor-quality dogs generally found in pet shops or the mixed breeds found everywhere. For poor-quality purebreds and mixed breeds have a hard time finding a home in this status-conscious society, which destroys twenty-five million pets each year in the United States alone. The shelters are *full* of wonderful, loving pets—both purebreds and mixes—who will die in the decompression chambers for lack of homes.

Owners of toy dogs should know that for the small bitch, whelping a litter presents great difficulty, often requiring a caesarean followed by a good deal of veterinary care. All too often, such bitches die while whelping, leaving the owner to wonder whether it was worth losing a beloved pet in order to have a couple of puppies—without a mother to feed them.

So consider wisely. And in doing so, think of your *dog*, not your own sexual hangups.

5
Do Spare the Rod

PUNISHMENT (as Distinguished from Correction)

I can't stress too often that *you*, the owner, by doing things correctly to begin with, can establish an environment in which punishment is unnecessary because mistakes do not occur. However, recognizing that you probably won't be perfect, I'll tell you how to punish.

If your dog makes a housebreaking or chewing mistake (no other circumstances call for "punishment"—"correction" perhaps, but not "punishment") no matter how much later you discover it, take him over to it, point out the error—he already knows it's there, of course—and jerk *hard* on the live ring of his training collar, while expressing disapproval in *very strong terms*. Then just drop the subject and ignore him for half an hour or so, unless it's the kind of mistake that requires a lot of cleanup work on your part. In that case, have the dog sit and stay in front of you while you clean up, and berate him in disgusted tones while applying the elbow-grease.

This is the closest we humans can come to the chastising a dam (mother) gives her pups when she shakes them and growls at them when they misbehave. But it will do if by obedience training you have already established yourself as pack leader and the collar as an authority symbol. More on these subjects in later chapters.

Keep in mind that when punishing a dog, hard as it may be not to get furious with him, you must remain aloof and *cool*. Don't lower yourself to his emotional level or he will be punishing *you!*

A word of caution on punishment. Most prospective clients say something like, "I've been beating the shit out of him for six months and that hasn't worked, so I'm ready to try something else." No, it hasn't worked. And never will.

For one thing, a dog will behave well only if *positively* motivated. Hitting a dog or even threatening him with your hand, a rolled paper, a stick, or whatever (who wants to go through life with a rolled newspaper in his hand?) actually will in the long run teach the dog to fight back. In other words, there will come a day when your dog, upon seeing that raised arm, will say in effect, "Dammit, I've been hit 418 times already, and that's enough!" and attack out of fear and self-defense. Worse yet, some small child raising his arm to throw a ball innocently sets off this reaction and gets hurt. You certainly can't blame the dog. It was the master who taught him aggression in *exactly the same way an attack dog is taught to kill*.

If you have been punishing your dog more than you have set up and rewarded good behavior, you may have created a masochistic dog, one who enjoys severe physical punishment and misbehaves in order to get it. Actually, he simply prefers negative attention to no attention. Yes, you'll say he gets lots of attention—petting, walks, play, and so on. But this is not the dog's idea of attention. He needs and wants structure.

You can correct the dog's masochistic behavior by changing your own behavior. Eliminate all situations in which the dog can do anything to displease you (see the following chapters). Do lots of precise obedience work accompanied by lavish praise. And if the dog does err, simply jerk on his collar a couple of times while expressing your displeasure, and then drop the subject. *Don't* lose your temper and carry on, thus giving the dog a great deal of negative attention and reducing yourself to his level. (Then who's punishing whom?)

6
Dogs Are Simply Not Altruistic

WHAT MAKES A DOG PROTECTIVE

It is generally recognized that bitches (females) are protective of their homes and dogs (males) protective of their owners. But those beliefs are oversimplified and require some explanation.

First of all, you must understand why dogs protect. It certainly is not because someone loves them; most dogs are loved. It certainly is not because someone feeds them; all dogs are fed. It certainly is not because they live in a certain house (which they protect); all our dogs live somewhere.

Rather, dogs protect the people they *relate* to and the homes in which those people live. The word "relate" here indicates that the dog thinks of himself and the person as a team, a unit in which *both* will be injured if *one* is injured. In other words, dogs are not altruistic. They do not protect out of love, but out of fear. If they believe something will harm them, they will protect themselves—and the person to whom they relate, who is part of the same unit.

This feeling of togetherness, which results in protectiveness, is best created by obedience training to a high level of performance. Some people achieve the same result because of their natural talent for making the dog their alter-ego (in a healthy sense of the word). But for most of us, a high level of obedience training is the best way. Most important: the obedience training must be achieved by the *positive* methods I'll outline here. A dog will not relate to, much less protect, a person who mistreats him. In fact, he may even side with the mugger!

Bitches seem to develop a high sense of premises protection at an early age, but this quality is natural to all dogs who relate to the people who live in the house. Don't expect your dog to bark at the doorbell or sounds near the house until he is at least seven months old. But if protectiveness is particularly important to you, rush the dog to the door with you whenever the doorbell rings, and say "Who's there?" in a tone that implies mistrust, wariness. Do the same whenever you hear a strange sound. When your dog begins to sense these dangers and runs to the door to listen, growl, or bark at unusual sounds, encourage him with, "Good boy," and continue saying, "Who's there?" in that scary tone.

Then once you ascertain the source of the sound and are sure it represents no danger, tell the dog. "Thank you, that's enough." And make him stop. Be sure he is under control before you open the door. A dog that barks at the door is one thing; a dog who attacks your best friend is another.

It is most important to recognize that your own attitude is the key to the dog's display of protectiveness. For instance, I live in a garden apartment in Manhattan and am understandably tense about strange noises. My Shelties bark at the drop of a pebble in the garden. As a result, the police are called and burglars are caught before they even have a chance to "case the joint." On the other hand, when I spend a weekend with friends who live on a high floor of an apartment building, I relax completely (how many burglars come in through a twentieth-floor window?) and the dogs bark only if someone rings the bell. They don't notice the sounds of people walking in the hall any more than I do, nor should they.

What of "attack training?" The real thing, security training, is done for police departments, the armed services, and similarly necessary situations. The "attack trained" dogs advertised for sale in most metropolitan areas are not security trained, but often are very sloppily (and cruelly) trained dogs that will probably be as lethal to their buyers as to a would-be burglar. For very easily understood reasons.

Start by recognizing that a security-trained dog is at least as dangerous as a loaded gun with the safety off. He must be very highly trained and under total control every second of the day and night. Very few people have legitimate need of a dog like this any more than they have of a loaded gun with the safety off. The only person who can maintain the proper degree of control over such a dog is a person who has trained with him throughout the training process, somebody who is totally emotionally stable, who does not drink (controlling any dog when you've been drinking is almost impossible), does not take drugs, and does not even get overtired. The dog must be worked with daily on obedience training and kept at a high level of obedience at all times. The "attack trained" dog and casual owner (that guy who calls our office every so often to ask, "How much will it cost to attack-train my six-week-old German Shepherd?") do not fit into this picture.

In addition, only a very small percentage of dogs are suitable for security training. The breed is not particularly important, but the temperament of the individual dog is. He or she must be completely even-tempered, friendly, outgoing. Never fearful or aggressive. One top security trainer who breeds dogs as well as training for many police departments often states that even starting with dogs he has bred and knows well, he is apt to discard nine or ten dogs along the way for each one that arrives at a point in the obedience training (the first step) where he feels he can proceed to security work.

7

The Dog Owner's Authority Symbols

TRAINING EQUIPMENT

What equipment do you need for training your dog? Not much. First buy him a proper training collar, one made of nylon with a metal ring at each end. Buy the smallest size that will fit over his head so as to prevent his chewing the collar or putting his feet through it. If your dog turns out to be the type to chew his collar, buy a flat-chain training collar. But then go to nylon the minute the chewing problem is licked. (Chain will shear off the coat around his neck, and chain collars seem to break more often than nylon collars.

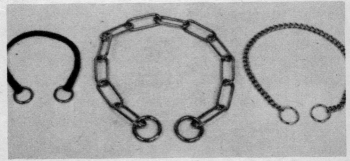

Three kinds of collars (left to right): nylon training collar, chain training collar, and fur-saver collar.

Nylon training collar is formed into this correct "p" shape by pulling nylon webbing through "dead" ring. Note that license, rabies tag, and ID tag are taped together to avoid noise.

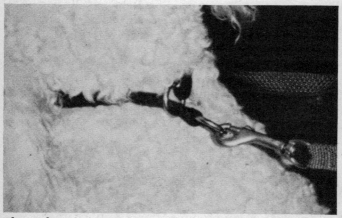

This is the proper way to put nylon training collar on your dog. Then collar releases correctly.

Also, it is almost impossible to get a good correction with a chain collar; it keeps slipping down his neck onto his shoulders. By the time you get it back up where it belongs, he has heard the "clinks" and knows what's coming. And you lose again!)

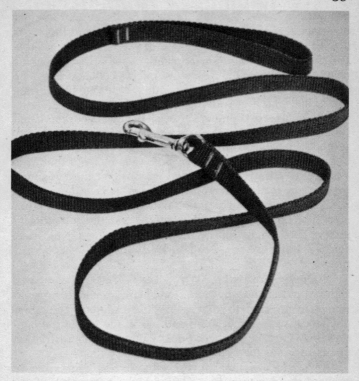

The six-foot nylon training lead with snap bolt. Resist temptation to buy a wider lead.

The collar is put on in the shape of a letter "p" when you are facing the dog. License, Rabies tag, and ID tag are attached to the dead ring and taped together to avoid noise. It is important that the collar be put on properly so that it releases correctly. If you are working with a long-haired dog, loosen the collar occasionally. The need for loosening will decrease as training progresses and corrections are less frequent.

You also need to buy a proper six-foot training lead. It should be made of webbed canvas or nylon. Do not buy a lead more than 1 inch wide. A wider lead may look very "macho," but it will be tremendously awkward. And awkward is never macho. Leather leads are satisfactory except that many dogs like the taste of them, and there you are with a chewing problem again. If you will be required to tie the dog during housebreaking (see Housebreaking chapter) also buy a cheap leather buckle collar and a cheap chain (unchewable) lead for use only while tying him during this initial phase of training.

At the outset of training, establish firmly in your mind and then in your pet's that the lead and collar are *your* authority symbols. It will be some time (and work) before you can begin commanding the dog by voice alone. Until then, the collar and lead are awfully important. So don't allow your dog to carry the lead in his mouth, and don't allow him to chew the lead or collar or to treat them disrespectfully in any other way. If he takes the lead in his mouth, grab the end quickly, jerk it hard, right out of his mouth, saying, "No!" very sharply. If you can't even call the lead your own, what hope is there?

Perhaps you're asking, "Why a lead?" The obvious answer is that you, the one who has most to learn, need it in order to remain connected to your dog while training. The other obvious answer is that more and more, the law of the land says dogs must be leashed. Society imposes this restriction for its own safety.

The world of animal lovers imposes the same rule to prevent the dog from being killed by an automobile, from running off and becoming lost, from jumping on and frightening a child or elderly person, from attacking another dog, and from eating a poisonous substance or a simple chicken bone. Occasionally my colleagues and I encounter someone who tells us the dog should be "free"—presumably this means free to die under the wheels of a car. No, those wonderful dogs who guide the blind do *not* make their way through traffic, following signs and lights. Generally they and their charges wait for some kindly sighted person to help them across. After all, the dog, no matter how well-trained, still has the mentality of a four-year-old child. How many parents send their four-year-olds to cross the street alone—"play in traffic,"as the saying goes?

Some people will tell you quite specifically: "Golden

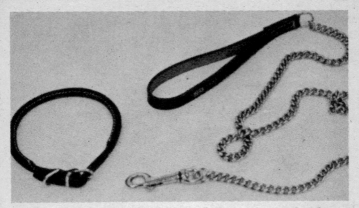

Buckle collar and chain lead are used if you must tie dog during housebreaking.

Retrievers were meant to run through the fields with abandon. They weren't intended to do all this precision drill." Weren't they? Ask the hunter, the person who trains hours on end in the hope of being able to take his dog into the field and have it obey rather than run out impulsively and flush the game prematurely. If the hunter's dog were not trained, the game would be gone before the hunter could blink an eye. And do you think the sheepdog herded the sheep when and where *he* pleased? Not likely.

So if you're still working out your own discipline concepts and can't quite come to grips with the many faces of "freedom," let's make a reasonable agreement: your dog will stay on lead through the training stages described in this book, leading to off-lead work. Once you and your dog have reached the off-lead stage and have completed your first AKC obedience title, that of Companion Dog, you can make an informed decision. By then, you will know that your dog is totally reliant upon your knowledge and awareness and can be "free" only whenever you are "perfect."

To answer another question you may be asking: No, the training collar (or slip collar) will not hurt the dog. His neck is quite strong and very different from yours. For instance, when you handle a human infant, you must support his head

Nylon training collar should be up high on neck to control a particularly rambunctious or large dog.

carefully; his neck is not strong enough to do so. But the youngest puppy is able to hold his head up, even before he can see. And from early on, his mother carries him around by the neck and disciplines him by shaking him by the neck. The pups gnaw on each other's necks and toss each other around that way. The base of the dog's neck, where it becomes shoulder, is so strong, in fact, that a collar resting there is totally ineffective. When you're dealing with a particularly rambunctious or large dog, you must be sure to keep the training collar up high on his neck, right behind his ears and immediately under his jaw.

Have you ever wondered about the harnesses you occasionally see on dogs accompanying "little old ladies in tennis shoes" (a term lovingly applied to many humane workers, whether male or female)? Those harnesses are simply the result of misunderstanding. They are generally used by people who cannot remember which ring of a training collar is attached to the lead (if you attach the lead to the "dead" ring, the collar doesn't tighten and the dog can walk out of it) or who don't know how to put a buckle collar on so that a dog can't slip out of it by pulling his head through it (you simply fasten it tightly enough that it won't go over the dog's head). Unfortunately, the harnesses sold in pet shops are most uncomfortable and frequently do permanent harm by forcing dogs to walk unnaturally. Proper harnesses for dogs that pull carts or guide blind persons or engage in tracking, backpacking, or sled pulling are specially made and used only for those purposes, not for training.

If physical defects in the vertebral discs of your dog's neck or in the formation of his windpipe cause your veterinarian to suggest a harness, take care to get a proper fit because a poorly fitting harness can cause problems of its own. Generally speaking, however, there is no place for a harness in the wardrobe of the healthy young dog you will be training.

Since the training collar and lead will be used for the rest of your dog's life, do get him his favorite color. And don't forget to wash them occasionally. Also, remember that his training collar and lead must *never* be left on when you leave him at home or when he is out of your sight, lest he hang himself. There may be times when you *feel* like strangling him, but you don't really mean it.

8
Your Betsy-Wetsy Dog

HOUSEBREAKING

Before you can learn *how* to housebreak, you must define "housebreaking" and come to grips with the basic facts of nature.

"Housebreaking" means to teach a dog to urinate and defecate in the street, in a corner of the yard, on his newspaper, or any other place *you* choose.

If your dog were living in his natural state, "housebreaking" would happen naturally. He would sleep one place (his den), he would play elsewhere, and he would urinate and defecate outside the areas of sleep and play. But your dog is not living in his natural state; he's living in your man-made environment, your living room, to be precise. So *you* must make the environment work right.

First, decide whether you want your dog to use paper, the street, or your yard. You may not teach more than one at a time. Most puppies are paper-trained because they may not go outdoors until they're about twelve weeks of age, after they've had the final Distemper-Hepatitis-Leptospirosis inoculation. Then they may be outdoor trained. But as soon as you begin outdoor training, all papers must go! Expecting the dog to use both paper and outdoors interchangeably is confusing and therefore cruel. (Yes, a twelve-week puppy can wait all day while you are out.) Outdoor training usually means better housebreaking because it provides no excuse for doing *anything* in the house *ever!* So choose the method carefully *before* you begin, and stick with it.

Before you go further, go back and reread the chapters on health and diet. You cannot expect to housebreak successfully if you do not make sure your dog is in good health and follow diet instructions exactly.

Now, let's come to grips with the realities of nature. Your dog—like all living beings—excretes: he urinates and defecates. Often clients cannot bear to use these words and instead use all kinds of euphemisms. Well, get down to the nitty-gritty because that's what is going to be on the rug if you don't. If you just cannot bear to use explicit words, don't expect to get very far with explicit acts!

Above all, don't use words that cover all subjects: "go to the bathroom," "go potty," "make," "mess," on and on, ad nauseum. Use words—preferably urinate and defecate—that indicate the function involved so that you can communicate effectively with others in the house. After all, if you take the dog out, he urinates, you rush in to answer the phone and tell your son the dog "made," he won't know that he should take him back out to finish—defecate, that is. But somebody will have to clean up, and it should be the one who didn't make things clear.

Which leads to another rule of dog training: "He who causes the accident shall clean it up, and he who causes the accident shall be the object of even more chastisement than the dog—poor creature."

Get organized for housebreaking. Start by reading the instructions through several times. Then follow them exactly, step by step. Remember, your dog was born perfect. All you need do is get your own head together. And miracle of miracles, you will find the method works and is much less work than cleaning up continually. Indeed, you can even return to going barefoot around the house!

Depending upon your choice of method, read either the outdoor section or the paper-training section. And simultaneously start the obedience work, no matter what age the dog.

You will see that with the passing of a few days, as the dog indicates through the obedience training that he is willing to take responsibility for his own behavior, his housebreaking will also be reliable. I never encounter a dog whose obedience is good and housebreaking poor, or vice versa—at least, not of his own will. If his obedience is good and housebreaking bad, look to yourself and what you are doing with his diet, schedule of walking, rewards and praise. If his housebreaking is good, on the other hand, the obedience lags, you are simply not effective enough in the training. That's a sign you should reread the obedience instructions and follows them all.

FORTY-EIGHT HOURS TO SANITY

Outdoor Housebreaking

In choosing to train your dog to use the outdoors, you have chosen to have him urinate and defecate in the part of the world you share with other people.

If he is to use your back yard, choose a place that can be cleaned up easily, and do clean up daily. If you want a compost heap, fine. But at least put it all in one place. Neighbors don't enjoy looking out a window to see a yard full of shit.

If you live in a city, plan to train your dog to use the *street*, not parks, sidewalks, bus stops, crosswalks, or tree areas, all of which are illegal in most areas anyway. In addition, if you teach your dog to use the park (ugh!), you will then be stuck with going into the park after dark, in bad weather, and so on. Don't ever let your dog use grass until he has been street-trained for some months. (If you go to the country for weekends, use the driveway or road.)

If you live in a city that does not require clean-up, at least use areas that are most frequently cleaned while street-training. If your city has "alternate side" parking, walk your dog on the side to be cleaned soonest. Get him as far from the curb as traffic permits so that the feces will disappear with the traffic or under street-cleaning equipment.

If he has an accident on the sidewalk or in the park, clean it up! You can always find a piece of paper in a litter basket or gutter and push the shit into the street. But don't leave it on the sidewalk! If you do, it will give the non-dog lover further reason to dislike dogs. But we dog owners will know you're the culprit (spelled p-i-g).

Your dog's natural activity pattern provides the basis for housebreaking. If your dog were on his own, he would arise, go off to urinate and defecate, return to play and eat and play some more, and then sleep for a long period. You, as a dog owner, will simply repeat that pattern throughout the day, modifying the time periods as necessary to suit your life.

Housebreaking starts when you are getting ready for bed. During the first weeks of housebreaking, the dog should be tied to your bed at night. If he is teething, he should continue to be tied to your bed or to his own until teething is a thing of the past. Once the housebreaking is good and teething is over and done, he may be loose in your bedroom but with the door closed or a gate across it. Never let him roam at night. Most dogs have housebreaking accidents under such circumstances or get into other trouble since they are to all intents and purposes "alone" if you are dead to the world.

Chances are that you are starting outdoor training with a puppy or adult dog that is more or less paper-trained. Let him urinate and defecate on the paper as late as he wishes. Then put the tying lead and collar on (see Equipment section), tie him to your bed with just enough lead to lie down, no more. He will not urinate and defecate when tied for a reasonable period.

Take up his papers and clean the spot thoroughly. It is best that he not be able to go near that spot again for a week. Put a chair over the spot, shut the door to that room, or do whatever is necessary to keep him away from that spot. Remember that in all probability he was "place-trained," not paper-trained. (If by any misfortune, his paper was in the only room you can use as his den, at least put something— wastebasket or his bed—in the area he usually used as a toilet so as to make it less accessible. And cross your fingers.)

Go to bed *dressed* in some old comfortable clothes. Put near your bed your shoes, your house keys, infant suppositories, small pieces (no bigger than a dime) of liverwurst (or cheese if liverwurst doesn't turn him on) wrapped in foil or plastic, a jacket for you if the weather's cold, and his obedience lead and collar.

Then go to sleep. But whether he awakens you in the early dawn or you have to awaken him at normal rising hour, get moving fast! Into your shoes and jacket. Pick up the dog (just unbuckle the collar), shove your keys, liverwurst, and suppositories into a pocket, put his obedience lead and collar on him, and *carry* him to the place he's to urinate and defecate.

Plan to carry your dog out for at least the first week—longer if he is very young. (Later in his training you can walk the puppy out only at a time that's not too long after the previous walk. In other words, the first walk of the day is *not* the time to try walking him out. Unless you like rewaxing your kitchen floor or cleaning up the elevator while half a dozen other tenants and doormen stand around clucking. Only when your dog has got into the habit of walking out on his midday walks and has demonstrated good "holding power" should you try walking him out for the first walk of the day.)

Put him down in the appropriate place, *walk him back and forth in a quick, businesslike manner*—no stopping for him to sniff; it's not necessary. Stay in a small area that will be convenient for you. Don't go around the block or all over the yard. (If your dog is to use your yard and it is fenced-in so he cannot run off, take him for the first couple of weeks to the spot you want him to use. Thereafter, let him out and he will *probably* go there. If he doesn't, go back to walking him there on a lead again. Most importantly, reward him immediately. Stand and watch him and be appreciative! After all, you can stand inside on a cold wet day. He has to traipse off to his privy.)

You're both there for business, not sightseeing. As you know, first thing in the morning he has to urinate and defecate and will indeed do so shortly. The moment he does either, reward him with a piece of liverwurst and *lavish praise*. If he has been out for a while and urinates but doesn't defecate, give him a suppository and walk him some more, quickly. If he is a large breed or very stubborn, use more than one suppository, in fact, as many as you need to (it's not unusual to use eight adult suppositories for an adult Shepherd). *He must defecate. Do not go in until he does.* Using the suppository gives you the opportunity to communicate your intent and pleasure quickly, so do use it.

Please don't make the mistake one of my clients did. When I called to check on the housebreaking, she said the dog still wasn't defecating when and where desired. When I asked whether she was using the suppositories, she replied, "Of course. I cut one up in her food every morning and she eats it okay, but nothing happens." No, no, no! It goes in the other end!

After your dog has urinated and defecated, do a couple of minutes of obedience training and go in. He may now have his "free" period, the length to be determined by age; read on. Set a timer based on the time he *urinated* so you keep track of the "free" period and don't extend it or he will have accidents. (For example, if his free period is twenty minutes and he urinates at 7:15, when you go in at 7:25—ten minutes later—set the timer for ten minutes.) During his free period, *keep lead and collar on, dragging, and keep him in sight so you can prevent trouble—like chewing plants or urinating while running around.* The lead is for your convenience as well as being an authority symbol. It is not a "ball and chain." Your dog, fortunately, doesn't project in those terms.

At the end of his free period, feed and water him. Then take him wherever you are and tie him near you on a fairly short lead. Or if you are going out, put him in his den. Give him a beef-hide toy in case he isn't sleepy.

If the puppy is quite young, he will need to go out soon again. After that walk, he may have a free period before being tied. Or he may be confined and left for the day if you go off to work.

You repeat this pattern of (a) urinate and defecate, (b) play and work, (c) confine or tie, throughout the day during the housebreaking period. Gradually you lengthen the free periods as the obedience progresses and the puppy matures. Finally you reach the point where your dog is left in his den only when you are out and he doesn't need to be restrained when you are home.

I'll give you some schedules for different ages of puppies and different life styles of owners. Choose the appropriate one, and stick to it until your dog is well housebroken.

If a housebreaking mistake has the effect of putting a puppy off schedule, you will find it easy to get him back to the timetable you desire. Simply hold him in your lap until the next scheduled walk. It is also possible to tie him *tightly* and *closely* to achieve this purpose, but holding him is more pleasant for both of you, and therefore more successful.

When you're housebreaking a young dog whose schedule must be carefully maintained, you will find it particularly helpful to keep a written record of how things go. Then if mistakes are made, you will be able to tell whether they are the result of human forgetfulness, the dog's inability to wait as long between walks as you had thought, or extraneous elements that you must control in the future.

For instance, if you have worked out a schedule that calls for walking the dog at 11:30 a.m., but your written record indicates that for two days running, the dog had an accident at 11:00 a.m. when the postman arrived, you'll realize that the dog should be walked before the postman arrives until he is old enough to control his bladder during periods of excitement. The written record should indicate everything that happens: when he urinates, defecates, eats, drinks water, or anything else of relevance. Keep the schedule in blue or black with mistakes entered in red so that they stand out immediately. You will quickly correct your mistakes and derive a good deal of satisfaction from a schedule that runs for pages with no red entries.

If there are errors, be sure to differentiate between accidents (your fault) and incidents (deliberate on his part). Accidents can be handled by a little more planning and attention. Incidents can be handled by more effective obedience work. A typical written record is shown here for your guidance. You will note both errors were accidents—the owner's fault.

Once your dog learns that the outdoors is his bathroom and that he gets rewarded for performing there, he will do

Date & Time	What U, D^s, F, W	Comments (Mistakes in Red)
Sat. 2/1		
7:30am	U + D	
8:15	F + W	
8:30	U	I forgot to tie after free period
12:05 pm	U	
4:00	U + D^s	
5:00	F + W	Much water
8:10	U	
11:45	U + D	
Sun. 2/2		
8:05am	U + D	
8:30	F + W	Teething – didn't eat much
12:30 pm	U	
1:00	D	Didn't stay out long enough
4:10	U	
5:15	F + W	
7:45	W	
8:00	U	
11:30	U + D^s	

Form in which to keep record of housebreaking schedule of an outdoor trained dog.

U-Urinate
D-Defecate
D^s-Defecate with aid of suppository
F-Food
W-Water
Boldface (in red on your chart) indicates mistake in house

something—at least urinate—every time he goes out, even every two hours. So you can "empty him out" whenever you want to leave him alone for a long period or when you want to play with him or take him visiting or shopping. He won't linger unnecessarily in the rain either.

If you have a male dog, you may wonder about his lifting his leg to urinate or the need to sniff. (Bitches rarely lift their legs to urinate against objects or need to sniff.) Leg-lifting and sniffing are territorial in nature and may appear in the unneutered dog as sexual maturity nears. They are not necessary to urinating and should be discouraged by not letting the dog stop to sniff and not taking him near vertical objects or tires on which other dogs have urinated. There is no need for him to put his face and whiskers in all that muck. What's worse, the dog who is so insecure that he wishes to do a lot of territorial marking (leg-lifting) outdoors will progress to doing it indoors. Let him continue to stand and urinate straight down—it's not "sissified," and it's normal for a secure dog.

Typical schedule for a three-month-old puppy on three meals a day with owner out of the house for a 9-5 work day, leaving home at 8:15 A.M. and returning at 6:00 P.M.

7:00 A.M.	Go out; urinate and defecate
7:30 A.M.	Food and water
7:45 A.M.	Tie
8:00 A.M.	Go out; urinate and defecate
	Into den for the day; leave no water for puppy to play in. But do leave toys and chewies
6:00 P.M.	Go out; urinate and defecate
6:30 P.M.	Food and water. Then tie
8:00 P.M.	Go out; urinate and defecate
8:30 P.M.	Tie
10:30 P.M.	Food and water while tied (small amount of water)
11:00 P.M.	Go out; urinate and defecate
	Tie when going to bed

Typical schedule for a three-month-old puppy on three meals a day with owner home on a flexible schedule.

7:00 A.M.	Go out; urinate and defecate
7:45 A.M.	Tie, then food and water
8:15 A.M.	Go out; urinate and defecate
9:00 A.M.	Tie
12:15 P.M.	Food and water while tied
12:45 P.M.	Go out; urinate and defecate
1:30 P.M.	Tie
5:00 P.M.	Food and water while tied
5:30 P.M.	Go out; urinate and defecate
6:15 P.M.	Tie
8:00 P.M.	Go out; urinate and defecate (this is an extra walk so that the puppy may have the pleasure of playing while the family is home in the evening; if the family were out, the puppy would be in his den)
8:45 P.M.	Tie
11:00 P.M.	Go out; urinate and defecate
	Tie when going to bed

Typical schedule for a five-month-old puppy on two meals a day and teething.

7:30 A.M.	Go out; urinate and defecate
8:00 A.M.	Food and water
	Into den if owner leaving; otherwise, tie at 9:30 A.M.

If owner home

12:10 P.M.	Water
12:30 P.M.	Go out; urinate
2:30 P.M.	Tie
6:00 P.M.	Go out; urinate and defecate
7:00 P.M.	Food and water
8:00 P.M.	Tie
11:00 P.M.	Go out; urinate and defecate
	Tie at night until teething is finished;

thereafter, keep in bedroom with
closed door or gate

**Typical schedule for a seven-month-old puppy on one
feeding a day.**

7:30 A.M.	Go out; urinate and defecate
8:00 A.M.	Food and water
	Into den if owner leaves for the day; otherwise, for the first few days of housebreaking, tie at 9:30 A.M. until next walk

If owner home

12:15 P.M.	Water
1:00 P.M.	Go out; urinate
	For the first days of housebreaking, tie at 3:00 P.M. until next walk
6:00 P.M.	Go out; urinate and defecate
	For first few days of housebreaking, tie at 8:00 P.M. until next walk; water while tied
11:00 P.M.	Go out; urinate and defecate
	Tie at night for the first few days of housebreaking; thereafter simply keep dog in bedroom with closed door or gate; if dog is still teething, however, keep tied until teething is over

Typical adult dog's schedule.

7:30 A.M.	Go out; urinate and defecate
8:00 A.M.	Food and water
	Into den if and when owner leaves for the day
5:00 P.M. (or whenever owner returns from work)	Go out; urinate and defecate

Water available

11:00 P.M.   Go out; urinate (and defecate if there
              have been housebreaking problems
              manifested by defecation during the
              night*)

OF COURSE YOU CAN PAPER-TRAIN
YOUR GREAT DANE, IF YOU HAVE AN EXTRA
SUNKEN BATHTUB

Paper-Training a Puppy

Paper-training obviously is suitable only for small dogs and puppies unable to go outside until receiving final inoculations. The sheer volume deposited by a medium- to large-size dog makes the very idea repulsive. No matter how lazy you are about walking your dog, you wouldn't enjoy using a shovel to clean up after him. Also, paper-training requires you to clean up promptly and completely.**

Most dogs have an inborn sense of cleanliness and will not use a soiled piece of paper. One of my own would use paper and then bark at me, demanding its immediate removal. And even if your dog hasn't heard that "cleanliness is next to godliness," the cockroaches have. If you don't clean up the papers and the floor under them (not carpeting, please!) very often and very thoroughly, the word goes out in the cockroach underground that a fallen angel has moved into 8C, and you will be inundated with the little creatures. Of course, if you also have a cat, he will be delighted, passing his days catching roaches. But that's not quite what you had in mind, is it?

So, in choosing the correct place for his papers, remember that this will be the place for the rest of his life. So choose

*Small dogs generally defecate twice a day; medium-size dogs defecate two-to-three times; large dogs defecate three times daily.

** Urine-soaked newspaper often reeks, but actually it is the newsprint that smells when wet even more than the urine itself. For that reason you might buy from a hospital supply house a quantity of bed liners, the sheets with plastic bottoms, absorbent tops. They are reasonably cheap by the gross and will eliminate a major source of odor.

well. One would-be client had rather unusual problems with paper. I found that she had placed the dog's paper in the kitchen doorway where anyone entering or leaving the kitchen had to step on it. I suggested we move the papers (and retrain accordingly) to a more convenient spot such as a bathroom, where it would be easy to clean the floor under the papers and people would not be stepping in a mess all the time. It was impossible to use a bathroom, she explained, because she used one bathroom herself (and evidently couldn't share it with the dog) and the *iguanas* used the other!

As the client explained this problem to me, I noticed the dog trying to get to the paper in the kitchen and the problem became obvious. The dog actually was beautifully paper-trained, but the door to the kitchen was closed. "To keep the cooking odors from escaping," I was told. The dog, in a state of panic, then ran into the den and used the zebra rug as a toilet. What with the cooking odors and iguanas, I guess the poor dog is still using the zebra rug. And what better way for a dog to express her indignation over the killing of another beautiful animal so that its skin might grace the floor.

Another client called to tell me that her kitchen ceiling had fallen in and that her dog, as a result, was ousted from his den while the ceiling was being repaired. Because the dog often snoozed in the bottom of her closet while she watched television, she moved his papers there. Wonder what her clothes smelled like . . .

And then there was the young woman who paper-trained her puppy on her bed, so she wouldn't have to get up to take him to his paper. So much for the blue satin comforter.

Any sort of housebreaking requires a good deal of patience and attention from you for the first few days. Thereafter, it is simply a matter of reinforcement. So make up your mind to put in the effort now and enjoy a well-trained dog later. And before even considering the mechanics of paper-training, you must accept the fact that providing your dog with what amounts to his own room is the first step and that success is impossible without it.

Lest you feel "confinement" is cruel, remind yourself again that dogs are by nature den-dwellers. They do indeed require space in which to run around, but for the greater part of the day they are content to stay in a small room and sleep. And confinement will protect your puppy from injury and your home from possible destruction. Puppies love to chew, and electrical wires seem to be a favorite—a lethal favorite, that is. Puppies are also unable to distinguish between unimportant pieces of furniture and the beautiful antiques you have gone to such pains to collect.

So select as his den a very small enclosed area such as a bathroom, part of a kitchen, dressing room, or whatever. Make sure it can be secured by doors or baby gates.

Now you are ready for the actual paper-training.

Put newspapers off to one side of the enclosed area so that the dog is not forced to be too close to his "toilet" if he wants to sleep or eat. Feed the puppy; give him water in a side dish. Hold him in your lap for about ten minutes. Then put him on the papers and hold him there with the collar and lead until he urinates and defecates.

If your dog does not defecate at the time you can reasonably expect him to, give him an infant suppository (available at any drugstore). If he doesn't defecate in a short time—such as ten minutes—give him another. Don't remove him from his paper until he defecates. The suppository has to work.

In case you can't quite believe this suggestion, let me assure you that you can use a suppository to train a dog just as many mothers do in toilet-training children. Simply insert the suppository all the way into the dog's rectum. No, it doesn't hurt. No, the dog doesn't associate the suppository with the act of defecating. The size of the infant suppository is appropriate for every dog from a Yorkie on up.

If you are paper-training a male dog, you will undoubtedly wonder whether he will or should lift his leg to urinate. The answer is no; that is, he probably won't and definitely shouldn't. Certainly, don't encourage him to do so by giving him one of those lovely red rubber fire plugs. And if he starts lifting his leg against the wall, move his papers out away from the wall or any other vertical object.

Remember, a male dog lifts his leg to urinate when he wants to leave his scent in order to dominate others. He certainly should not have a need to dominate other scents in his own home. If he does, get busy with that obedience work and don't stop until his obedience title is hanging on the wall and you can truthfully say, "I'm master. I dominate in this house." Leg-lifting in his own home, as an indication of a severe dog behavioral problem, is second only to aggression toward his master.

While holding your puppy on the paper, talk to him, softly, saying, "Use your paper, use your paper." When he defecates or urinates, praise him lavishly and give him a tiny piece of liverwurst, about the size of a dime. (If by chance liverwurst doesn't turn him on, try Swiss cheese or chicken.) Keep him in the area until he has urinated or defecated, as expected, no matter how long it takes! (I have seen an adult Yorkie hold out for twenty-seven hours, hoping finally to get back to the living-room carpet!)

After the puppy has urinated and defecated, take him out of the enclosed area and let him run around and play with you *with his lead and collar on,* lead dragging so you can catch him and return him to his paper if he starts to urinate or defecate on your rug. Keep him in sight at all times during this play period. After about thirty minutes from the time he urinated (less for very young puppies), *walk* him on his lead back to his area. The purpose in walking the dog back to his paper rather than carrying him, as you will tend to do with a small puppy, is that it teaches him how to get to his paper from anywhere in the house. And that is, after all, the ultimate goal of all your work.

If you are firm and have a positive attitude about his den, your puppy will sense it, and the matter will be quickly settled. Sometimes, however, an owner encounters a particularly stubborn and spoiled little fellow. When you confine him and leave the room, he will immediately start to whine, howl, or bark—perhaps all three. Anything to make you come back. Depending upon your living situation— apartment or private house—and your nerves, you can either ignore the racket until he gets tired, or you can proceed to correct the problem.

Correction involves making your immediate return to the room so dreaded that he will think twice before he pulls a tantrum. You can get your point across by entering the room quickly in an apparent fit of anger and yelling, "No!" again and again *sharply* and *firmly* as you shake your pup by the collar—just as the mother dogs discipline their pups. And mother dogs never get any back talk! Sharpness and firmness are most important—not physical strength—when disciplining a young puppy. You are molding his future behavior, and his first impressions of you are everything. Remember, much as you love him: he is the dog and you are the master.

Once you return the pup to his area after his half-hour of activity, he will probably sleep for several hours. It is normal for puppies to exercise wildly for about twenty to thirty minutes and then sack our for several hours. So why not take advantage of this normal body pattern? When he wakes up or you awaken him, put him on the paper at once. Tell him: "Use your paper, use your paper!" And when he urinates or defecates or both (young puppies defecate first thing in the morning and about half an hour after each meal; puppies over four months usually defecate first thing in the morning, late in the afternoon, and before bedtime), praise him and give him a dime-size piece of liverwurst as his reward. Again, let him out of his den to play, returning him to his area in half an hour.

The freedom period of thirty minutes also includes the work period, during which you do obedience training with your puppy. If you have trouble keeping track of time, buy a cheap stove-top timer. The minute he urinates, set the timer for the appropriate length of the freedom period. This period is gradually lengthened as the dog indicates his understanding of papertraining and as he becomes willing to assume responsibility, as evidenced by his obedience work.

For instance, after several days in which there have been no accidents during the dog's thirty-minute freedom period, lengthen that period to forty minutes. Several days later lengthen it to fifty minutes, and so on.

The "safe" time (during which he can control himself and not have accidents while running around) depends of course upon the dog's age. A puppy of six or seven weeks cannot be depended upon for much more than twenty minutes; a puppy of twelve weeks can manage about half an hour to forty-five minutes; a puppy at five months of age can control himself for as long as two hours.

But let me add a word of caution: these freedom periods presuppose that you are supervising him at all times. A puppy may not be out of sight and must have his lead dragging until his training is quite advanced. Otherwise, he may not only have housebreaking accidents but may also chew anything and everything. Any time you cannot watch him, if you will simply be present but occupied (such as while cooking or watching television), tie his lead to your chair or some nearby piece of furniture. If you are leaving the house, even for a minute, put him back in his den area, securely enclosed. And remember, he will live in this den when you are out for the rest of his life.

If he has an accident while playing, take him to the spot, show it to him, letting him smell it, but not pushing his face into it, and scold him while jerking on his collar. Then take him to his area and put him on the paper, saying, "Use your paper, use your paper." In all probability he will *not* use the paper because he just used your carpet. So simply leave him in his area and ignore him for a while. He will probably sleep, so be prepared for the after-sleep routine when he awakens.

Obviously, a very young puppy needs to sleep in his den area at night because he will use the paper during those hours. At 12 weeks of age, however, he may begin to sleep in a bedroom with people, but tied closely to the bed so that he cannot roam and make mistakes. He must be put on his papers the minute you arise or he awakens you. Once he is safely beyond the teething age, he may be free in the bedroom at night, but do close the door or put a gate across the doorway so he can't wander.

Your use of praise and reward will have the result, quite quickly, that your puppy will look up to you happily, wagging his tail, as he uses his paper. He wants and expects his praise and reward. Don't ever disappoint him!

When it has become obvious that your puppy knows he will be praised and rewarded for using his paper, you no longer must walk him to it or keep the lead on all the time. Supervise him sufficiently to be sure he gets back to his paper, and say, "Use your paper." Then wait for him to do so, and give him praise and reward.

If you find him running off into corners to make mistakes out of your sight, put the lead back on him for a day or so. But also, please don't ever shut the door between him and his paper. That's not fair!

If occasionally he doesn't bother using his paper, that's his way of getting your attention or testing you; you are beginning to take his good behavior for granted. If he is more than a few inches from the paper, treat the incident as a housebreaking mistake, scolding him and putting him on his paper and saying, "Use your paper, use your paper." And work on his obedience more often and more firmly. If he's not responsible for performing well in obedience training, he certainly won't be responsible for his housebreaking!

With a little more work and patience on your part (also called self-discipline), you will soon have a puppy who makes the effort to return to his paper when necessary. And after doing so, he will come to tell you what a good boy he has been—in full expectation of seeing you stand on your head with joy! So praise and reward him.

Paper-Training a Mature Dog

Occasionally, when an owner becomes incapacitated to the point of being unable to walk his dog or the dog becomes unable to move about and walk easily, it is necessary to paper-train a mature dog accustomed to going outside. This is not difficult, nor is it cruel. The dog would much rather stay with his beloved master—paper-training and all—than have to find a new home or, worse yet, be euthanatized (that charming euphemism for "killed").

Just get to work and paper-train him with an attitude that makes it clear to the dog that both you and he have something to work out and that you are prepared to be patient and make an effort. The job can easily be done in forty-eight hours.

Read the foregoing instructions for paper-training a puppy. The obvious difference is that the mature dog will sit with his papers, able to wait long periods of time without urinating or defecating, expecting you to take him out. So start in the morning, and don't get dressed. Stay in your pajamas. You know how excited he gets when you give signs of being dressed to take him out. So don't.

Instead, when you get up in the morning, take him to the place you have chosen for his area and his papers (preferably the bathroom or another similar *small*, washable room) and put lots of paper down for him. Then close him and yourself in there. Give him a suppository (probably several will be required, since he will resist at first), so that he is forced to do something soon. When he does, you have the opportunity to reward him immediately with a piece of liverwurst and lots of praise, *lavish praise!* (The importance of using the suppository cannot be overemphasized; it gives you the *immediate* opportunity to communicate your intention and then your pleasure at his complying.) When this happens, he will be quite surprised and rather delighted, having expected to be punished for defecating in the house.

Now just sit there in his small room with him, give him his breakfast and plenty of water, and then wait until he has to urinate. It may be hours.

Meantime you can certainly leave him there for a few minutes at a time to do your own chores. But keep coming back to him so that the minute he urinates—from sheer necessity—you're on hand to provide the liverwurst and the praise again. It may take as long as twelve to fourteen hours, a total of twenty-four to twenty-six hours since his last outside walk. *But don't give up. Just wait it out.*

Also, don't act as if you must be punishing him. He may be confused for the first forty-eight hours or so, but nothing worse than confused. After he has urinated (and previously defecated from the suppositories), let him out of his area to play with you. He can be out with you, under supervision, of course, for about ten hours. If it's time for you to go to bed, you can maintain your supervision of him by tying him to *your* bed or *his* to sleep. He won't mind if he's accustomed to sleeping there anyway. Then when you arise, walk him to his papers and repeat the routine. *Continue the supervision and rewards for at least ten days, and longer if necessary.*

All it takes is lots of love and patience, and you will have a happy, paper-trained companion able to remain with you despite your or his inability to walk normal distances. As every housebound person can tell you, this is the time you need your dog most, and also a time when the dog will most enjoy the closeness of his master.

9
Obedience Training

In reading other chapters of this book, you frequently see references to obedience training. It seems to be part of the cure for every problem. And indeed it is.

Obedience training is not an end in itself. It is certainly a convenience for the dog owner, an important safety factor for the dog, and a reassurance to society as a whole. But in this book I most often regard obedience training as a form of therapy that's useful in establishing an appropriate relationship between owner and dog, a relationship that is central to the dog's mental health and your own peace of mind as well as to all problem-solving.

If you are serious about getting into obedience work, do so in an organized form, following the instructions to the letter. Unbelievable as it may seem to you at this point, your dog *will* know the difference between precise work and sloppy work and will judge you accordingly—basing his relationship with you upon this judgment.

If you will think about the different dog breeds for a moment, you will realize that once upon a time most of them were bred for a specific purpose. The work that was originally demanded of a Retriever or a Shepherd was far more demanding than anything you are likely to impose upon your dog. But obedience training will just have to do unless you plan on keeping sheep or hunting ducks. The obedience work will, however, fulfill your dog's need to be useful as well as giving you the opportunity to assume the role of pack leader.

The traditional obedience work has arisen from the original position of the dog as man's companion. It is for this reason that the basic obedience title that may be earned in obedience trials is that of "Companion Dog." The dog who earns this title is truly a fit companion for man.

During the initial period of obedience training, you will need to have specific training sessions each day, as well as using the training whenever you deal with your dog. I recommend that when you work with a puppy between seven weeks and four months of age, you work about five to ten minutes at a time, several times a day, rather than pushing through long training periods. Be sure to keep things light and encouraging for a young puppy—no pressure, please!

Puppies over four months of age may work for periods of twenty to thirty minutes a day. The average dog of seven months or more can work for considerably longer periods of time. After all, if he were out herding sheep or working the field, he would be at it all day. Be sure, however, that every session ends on a positive note. If he's not doing a command well, work on it. But then go on to something he does well and end with that.

Each command has a purpose and is well within the dog's ability. It is most important that as fast as possible, you start using the obedience work in daily routines so that it becomes a way of life. A trained dog *always* heels; when he goes visiting, he *always* downs and stays at his owner's heel until released; when seeing a veterinarian, he *always* stands for examination on the table. The obedience work serves no purpose if it does not become habitual any more than teaching your children good manners serves any purpose if they use them only at home alone with you.

Anything you teach a young puppy and stick with will be with him the rest of his life. My dogs literally do not know that I have a right side (trained dogs walk on the left). They have *never* tripped me by darting between my feet or across my path. And of course, they have never been hurt by being stepped on or tripped over.

Your own enthusiasm will be the key to your dog's enthusiasm. He can be bored and unwilling to work only if you are. Talk to him constantly. Before beginning to teach any command, remember that you must *communicate* verbally, demonstrate physically, and then *praise*. Always in that order. DON'T TRY TO FORCE THE DOG TO DO ANYTHING UNTIL YOU HAVE GIVEN A COMMAND. THEN ENFORCE IT IMMEDIATELY; FOLLOW IT WITH PRAISE AND LOTS OF ENCOURAGEMENT.

As you work, praise him constantly. Show off his work to your friends and relatives—making sure they "ooh" and "ah" appropriately. It is quite normal for a dog to *demand* his daily obedience session by bringing his lead to you, barking furiously at the lead, or going to his training area and waiting for you. Encourage this attitude in every way possible. And your dog will be like the kid on the block who loves his arithmetic!

OBEDIENCE STANDARDS

Although many *methods* of training have been used over the years, the *standards* for obedience performance have been quite specific. Changes have always been toward even greater specificity. These standards are pretty much the same worldwide. But for this book, I have chosen to use those set forth by the American Kennel Club. Before I give instructions for an exercise, I'll precede them by the applicable part of the AKC's "Obedience Regulations, January 1, 1975."

However, it is neither possible nor necessary to reprint here the entire volume of obedience regulations. I won't be trying to teach all levels of obedience work included therein, but only those commands required for Novice Obedience work. In other words, I'll focus on what your dog must do to earn a Companion Dog title and to be a true companion to you.

Right now, obedience trials in the United States are open only to purebred dogs. This situation should surely change in the near future, since the dog's performance in the obedience ring depends upon his training and handling, not his breed.

I believe it's likely that you will enjoy reviewing the full form of the Obedience Regulations. You can get a copy free from the American Kennel Club, 51 Madison Avenue, New York, N. Y. 10010. AKC will automatically send you the most recently revised regulations.

When you write for the obedience regulations, you might also ask for a calendar of obedience trials so that you can attend one in your area. Obedience trials are held throughout the country every weekend and are attended by thousands of dog owners. I know: you're sitting there saying, "All I want to do is get the dog housebroken. Who cares about obedience trials?" Well, that's exactly what all those people at trials once said. Then as training progressed, they found they enjoyed it, the dog enjoyed it, and—as a team—they were a hit. Then someone invited them to watch a trial. And just like that, another training addict was born.

At any rate, watching an obedience trial will give you a good idea of what your dog is capable of, if you can just get *yourself* together. After watching a Pomeranian do a scent-discrimination exercise, you can hardly claim your shepherd will never learn to heel!

If you talk with some of the people at the trial, you will find that many of them belong to nonprofit obedience training clubs that are members of the American Kennel Club. These clubs generally offer obedience training classes at all levels of obedience work. Such classes will be particularly necessary to you if you go beyond the "Novice" level, since advanced work is best started in a class with a knowledgeable instructor. The names of these clubs, again, are available from the American Kennel Cub at the address just mentioned.

Lest you think this all sounds awfully "stiff," start your obedience training with this concept in mind: "Standard of Perfection. The judge must carry a mental picture of the theoretically perfect performance in each exercise and score each dog and handler against this visualized standard which shall combine the utmost in willingness, enjoyment and precision on the part of the dog, and naturalness, gentleness, and smoothness in handling. Lack of willingness or enjoyment on the part of the dog must be penalized, as much as lack of precision in the dog's performance, roughness in handling, military precision or peremptory commands by the handler."*

STARTING THE ACTUAL
OBEDIENCE WORK

How to Hold the Lead for Heeling Have you ever seen those people who walk around clasping their hands and muttering to themselves as they twist their wrists right and left, practicing their golf grip? Sports from archery to knitting require the novice to learn how to hold the appropriate equipment and then use it gracefully, with proper timing. Fortunately for dog owners, dog training is one of the easier sports. So don't despair just because after five years of tennis lessons you still haven't got your backhand together.

You'll begin dog training by using both hands on the lead. Eventually, just before you go to off-lead work, you will use only one hand (the right). The right hand is stationary on the lead; the left hand moves. Keep this in mind! And don't worry about whether you are righthanded or lefthanded; it matters not. Just follow the instructions exactly as they're written.

Now using a lead *without* a dog at the end, please, put the handle of the lead over your right wrist; don't hold onto it. Put your left hand *over* the lead at about midpoint; that is, grasp it from the top, not under the bottom. It is this hand-over-the-lead position that gives you *all* the leverage and the dog *none*. (This is so important that I suggest you write it on the hall mirror in soap so that you see it before going out each time.)

Now, hold your right hand in front of you, slightly cupped toward your body. Separate the index finger from the rest slightly and run the lead, the part between the handle and your left hand, over the index finger. The lead, at a point about two feet from the handle, will be looped over the index

* *Obedience Regulations*, January 1, 1975, New York: The American Kennel Club, p. 13, Section 2.

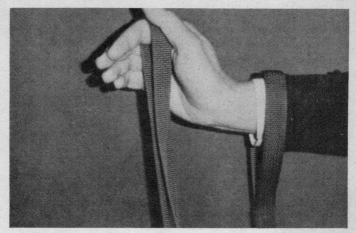

Right hand controls length of lead. Notice that "handle" is over wrist and that lead is then looped over index finger for holding within palm of right hand.

finger and held within the palm of the right hand—the stationary hand, remember?—for pure strength.

Next, practice letting your left hand, holding the lead lightly, drop straight down to your side naturally, while you hold your right hand (with the lead looped over your right index finger and the lead's handle over your right wrist) close to your body at waist height and relaxed. Your left hand will provide the specific guidance and correction (a quick jerk on the lead) as your right hand remains the anchor. When you jerk the dog in close, the lead will pass through your left hand and your right hand, moving upward and to the right, will take up the slack. When you want to let the dog out again, your right hand plays out more lead through your left hand. It's most important to carry your left arm loose and relaxed at your side so that it has room to move for correction, which is mostly a hard flick of the wrist. If you hold your left hand up and your arm tense, you'll have nowhere to go with a correction. And you'll have a sore left shoulder.

When you hold your arms relaxed and your hands as I've just indicated, your strength flows naturally with no effort, even it you're handling a two-hundred-pound dog. You won't build muscles—or need them—while training your dog!

Once you have become relaxed and natural with the lead, you may attach to it your dog and proceed.

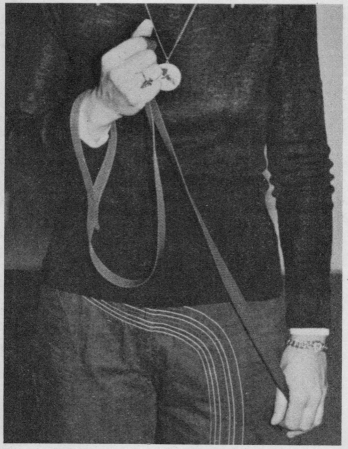

Let your left hand, placed over the lead lightly, drop straight down at your side naturally. Hold your right hand (with lead looped over index finger and handle over wrist as shown) close to your body, relaxed, at about waist height.

Sit Sometimes it's necessary for me to explain exactly what is meant by a command, but "sit" is pretty obvious.

With the collar and lead on your dog, take the lead as indicated for heeling. (The dog will end up toward your left side.) Say, "Superdog, sit!" A split second after issuing this command pull up on the collar and lead. If the dog is even with you or ahead, pull up and back; if he is a bit behind you, pull forward and then up. Release the tension on the lead the second the dog sits, and praise him. If he's a puppy or just generally "nutsy," he'll probably get right back up to receive his praise. That's perfectly normal. You're teaching sit—not stay—at the moment.

A split second after commanding the dog to sit, pull up on the lead and collar.

Pull up with your right hand, pushing the dog's rear end down with your left hand, repeating the command, "Sit."

Some dogs are very stubborn about sitting, and pulling up on the collar is not enough. (I know, you've just discovered yours falls into that category.) Give the command "sit." Then, as you pull up, take your left hand off the lead, leaving the right hand to manage that upward pull, and put your left hand on the dog's rear. Pull up with the right hand, push down with the left, repeating "sit," again followed by praise. You shouldn't have to use your hand to push his derrière down more than two or three times if you are communicating.

If you keep forgetting to say, "Sit," (that is, forgetting to tell him what he's supposed to learn) he will assume that

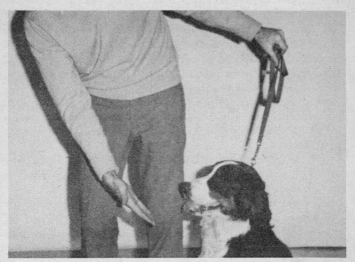

The hand signal for sit is an upward motion of the right arm, hand extended, palm up.

you're doing some kind of calisthenics in which you bend over him, pull up with your right hand, push down with your left, and then cheer yourself on. Please, let him know verbally that all this is intended for him.

After your dog has indicated some comprehension of the command, which he should do within the first five minutes or so, begin adding the hand signal at the same time. The hand signal for sit is an upward motion of your right arm, hand extended, palm up. (I've been told this is a very rude gesture in Italian neighborhoods, but your dog will never know.) If you combine voice and hand command, he will learn both and be able to function on either within a short time.

Lead-Training a Puppy It may seem to you that other people's dogs get lead-trained automatically and that somehow yours is an entirely different matter. And of course, if he *won't move*, you can hardly expect to do much else with him. Like housebreaking.

So let's begin at the beginning. Put a little lightweight training collar on him and let him walk around with it for a while, perhaps a half hour or so. Then attach his lead and let him drag that around for a bit. Then attach your hand to the other end of the lead and start walking around with him—if he walks, that is. Just follow the way he goes. After a bit of that, start chattering encouragingly while giving tiny tugs on the lead so that he realizes you are on the other end. Then give slightly harder tugs, still cooing. Start leading him around with these tugs. Yes, he's apt to resist, perhaps have a minor (or even major) temper tantrum. But most of that is for your benefit.

As you get him moving on the lead, try to keep him to your left. This will help when you teach formal heeling, which is· the obvious next step.

If you happen to buy a puppy that has been in a pet shop or elsewhere until the age of three months or more with *no* lead training whatsoever, expect a fight. And since you'll have to start housebreaking the minute you get him, try the following method. Get ready for your housebreaking, with all your supplies in hand and procedures in mind. *Carry* him outside (see Housebreaking instructions) and to the nearest ice-cream store. Get a good, drippy cone. Put your puppy on the ground in a safe area and push a little of the ice cream onto his mouth. He'll like it, to put it mildly. Then hold the ice cream cone in front of him as you walk along. It's a bit backbreaking, but it sure gets a puppy lead-trained in a hurry without a lot of screaming to awaken the neighbors.

And you get to finish the cone.

The Dog Who Is Accustomed to Walking His Master It would be madness to think you could start right in teaching your 180-lb. St. Bernard to heel when he has been walking (dragging?) you for the last three years, or ten years, or whatever. First you must teach him to remember that you are on the other end of the lead and then that you deserve a little respect.

So put on his training collar and lead, and take him where there is a good deal of space with no pedestrians or loose dogs. Grasp the lead in both hands as explained in the section on how to hold the lead for heeling.

As he heads over in some direction or other, just let him

go, bracing your feet firmly. Just a split second before he hits the end of the lead, give a jerk backwards so that he gets the force of hitting the end of the lead and your jerk backwards at the same moment. He will probably *fly* around and immediately head off in some other direction. Whatever way he goes, you go in the *opposite* direction *fast*, again jerking on the lead a split second before he hits the end.

After about half a dozen such experiences, he will begin to

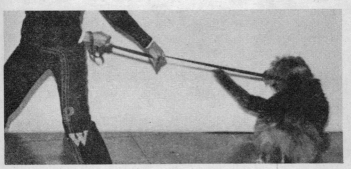

How to change the pattern of a dog who is accustomed to walking you: A split second before he hits the end of the lead, give a jerk backwards so that he gets the combined force of hitting the end of the lead and your jerk backwards.

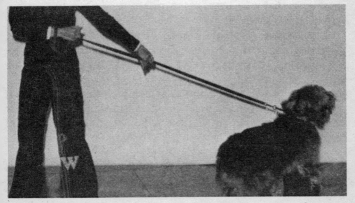

Whatever way the forging dog goes, you go in the opposite direction fast, again jerking on the lead a split second before he hits the end.

Two views of an owner with her dog walking properly at heel.

look at you warily. He will also stop hitting the end of the lead *so hard,* and then stop altogether. And if you are heading in the opposite direction fast enough, he'll be at your side, your left side because it is your left hand guiding the lead. Now you can start heeling lessons.

Remember this little exercise and use it every time you start a lesson until he gets so good that you don't need to remind him there's a human being at the other end of the lead and that you have some rights, too!

Heeling First, a look at some official words on heeling:

"Heel Position. The heel position as used in these regulations, whether the dog is sitting, standing, or moving at heel, means that the dog shall be straight in line with the direction in which the handler is facing, at the handler's left side, and as close as practicable to the handler's left leg without crowding, permitting the handler freedom of motion at all times. The area from the dog's head to shoulder shall be in line with the handler's left hip."*

"Heel on Leash & Figure Eight. The principal feature of this exercise is the ability of the dog and handler to work as a team."

*Obedience Regulations, January 1, 1975, Chapter 2, Section 18, p. 16.

". . . The dog shall walk close to the left side of the handler without swinging wide, lagging, forging or crowding. Whether heeling or sitting, the dog must not interfere with the handler's freedom of motion at any time. At each order to Halt, the handler will stop and his dog shall sit straight and promptly in the Heel Position without command or signal, and shall not move until the handler again moves forward on order from the judge."*

What all this translates to is that "Heel" means your dog stays on your left, moving at your pace, the tip of his nose even with your thigh, never pulling on the lead, and sitting automatically whenever you stop. The two of you are truly a team. It is natural for a dog, while heeling, to turn his head toward your left leg every few steps to check your position. He also should be able to find the heel position from anywhere. But that subject will be covered in a subsequent chapter.

Begin by taking the lead in your hands correctly and having Superdog sit straight at your left side head even with your knee. Hold the lead firmly, with your left hand dropping relaxed down your side. As you step forward, say, "Superdog, heel!" sharply and jerk the lead forward, letting up on the pressure instantly. The dog will probably either drag behind or leap forward ahead of you. If he drags behind, keep walking and jerk him gently forward into heel position, repeating, "Heel," sharply followed by some encouraging chit chat. *Don't keep the lead taut*. Let it go slack and tight, as you would playing a fish.

Stop occasionally, bringing your dog up to the heel position, having him sit, praising him greatly, patting him a few times. He will quickly get over his confusion and keep up with you. *Don't under any circumstances keep the lead tight; he will fight it and you will be wasting energy* and end up exhausted. And don't wait for him, or keep looking back at your dog. Just move out!

Then there's the dog who jumps up at your left side instead of moving with you. If yours does so, slide your left hand down the lead hard, almost to his neck, and tighten the

*Ibid., Chapter 3, Section 5, p. 21.

When the dog is heeling and you stop, the dog should sit automatically at heel.

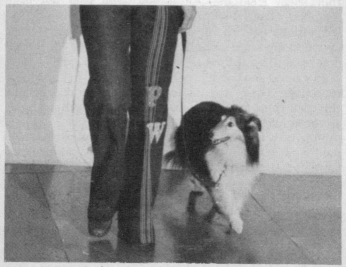

The dog trained properly to heel will turn his head occasionally toward handler's left leg to make sure of position.

If, instead of heeling, the dog decides to jump up at your side, slide your left hand down the lead hard, almost to the dog's neck, and tighten the collar swiftly. Tell him, "No!" and get back to work fast.

collar swiftly, saying, "No." Then just get back to work fast. Usually these jumping incidents occur because there is a void, a lack of command or action, and the dog fills it as best (worst?) he can.

More common is the dog who bounds ahead or just sneaks ahead of heel position. "Ahead" is anything at all ahead of your knee, be it half an inch or two feet. This maneuver on Superdog's part is called forging. *Don't tighten the lead. Don't incline your left arm backwards hoping by some miracle to keep him from rushing forward.* Rather, let the whole six feet of the lead go right out with him, make a fast right (clockwise) about-turn, and the split second you are headed away from him, give a *hard* jerk on the lead. Don't waste the energy throwing him forward all the way to your heel. The jerk will serve to let him know you're headed in the opposite direction, particularly if it is accompanied by a sharp, "Heel!" The second he catches up with you, reverse again *fast*.

Yes, I know you're getting dizzy. So is he. Accompany that sharp jerk on the lead, after you're headed the other way, with the command, "Heel!" and this time keep going. If he

If, instead of heeling, the dog forges ahead, resist temptation to tighten lead. Let the whole six feet of lead go right out with him.

After you let the six feet of lead go out with your dog, you make a fast right about-turn. The instant you are headed away from him, give a hard jerk on the lead. He'll start to get the message.

inches ahead, reverse again. *It is most important to keep the lead loose so as not to start a tug-of-war scene.*

Also, if the lead is tight, he doesn't have to *watch* where you go; he *feels* it. We want to have the lead so loose that the lead's snap bolt at the collar hangs *down*, rather than inclining up. The loose lead will force him to take responsibility for his activities instead of your doing all the work. And that's one reason for a lot of this obedience work: to get your dog to take over responsibility. No matter how many times you have to reverse, keep doing it until he drops back into the heel position.

The moment your dog catches up with you after your first about-turn, you reverse your direction again fast.

To correct forging (instead of heeling) by a large, quick-witted dog, you make a left about-turn, bringing your right knee into the dog.

A constant need for the hard reverse does not indicate a high degree of recalcitrance on your dog's part as much as poor timing on yours. When you make the reverse, your movement must flow directly. You must not be headed in one direction, notice that he forges, stop a second, and reverse direction. That process gives him plenty of time to check out the situation, and you gain nothing. You must teach yourself to move with him at heel, and as you notice him beginning to forge ahead, reverse instantaneously—just go!—bringing him flying after you. Make sure you give him that sharp jerk *after* you have headed in the other direction. Don't do him the favor of guiding him along with you. Let him find himself six feet from you, headed in the opposite direction. He should be terribly embarrassed. If he's not, you're not communicating very well.

If you have an extremely quick-witted large breed, he may begin to know when you are going to reverse and get himself into position before you can correct easily. So alternate right (clockwise) about-turn reverses with left (counterclockwise) U-turns directly into the dog. Now here's the hard part: coming into him with your left leg is not particularly effective. But if you can get yourself coordinated so that your left hand pulls him in toward you, a parallel motion, as you come around into him with your *right* knee, hard, fast, without pause, you will have one surprised dog. Alternating these about-turns, of course, is most important.

But remember, the correct about-turn in normal daily use (once your dog is trained) is made to the right so as not to run into the dog and cause all kinds of confusion on the sidewalks.

Adding the Sit As you begin to get things under control, start making frequent stops, saying "Sit" loudly and firmly a split second before you stop, so that he has time to react and sit as you stop. Make sure he sits straight at your side, parallel with the direction you're heading. Also, don't always walk in straight lines. Zigzag across the sidewalk, make little circles to your right and left. Make right turns and left turns at sharp angles. Walk very slowly, as if window shopping. Get your dog under control, and then pick up speed gradually until you are both running. Most dogs tend to start playing and getting out of control when running, but only because their owners allow them to. If yours begins to clown around, slow down immediately, saying, "Heel!" very sharply. Then when you're sure he's calmed down and under control again, start speeding up again until you're running. Then slow down again. Keep changing pace until your dog can do likewise quite automatically without losing his self-control.

If your little darling coyly and cleverly sits when you stop, but somehow sits behind you, catch him (as the accompanying photo shows) with your right foot behind you, at the same time bringing him forward into the heel position with the

If you stop and your dog sits behind you, catch him with your right foot behind you, at the same time bringing him forward into proper heel position with the lead.

lead. In fact, correct any sits that are not *perfectly* in heel position, and correct them with the lead. If you put your hands on the dog every time and do all the work for him, he'll *enjoy* the corrections and make even more mistakes.

As you are trying to remember all these instructions, there is another important point: be sure to give the heel command every time you start forward with your dog after a stop and sit. And as the teamwork between you and Superdog improves, you might start adding the hand signal for heel forward. It is a forward motion of the left hand, palm forward, over the dog's head. He'll just follow the hand and you forward at heel.

In all heeling work, it's most important for you to keep that lead *very loose* down your left side. Relax. Don't pull either arm up tight. And make those quick about-turns without stopping, giving the dog a hard jerk on the lead after you head the other way. The result of this about-turn, if done properly, is that the dog will never go ahead of you or fail to stop in a position that's even with your leg as you stop.

If your dog forges ahead or overruns you on stops, you're not making your about-turns effectively. Reread the instructions and proceed with it correctly! Your dog in the hands of an experienced handler would be perfect from the beginning. The practice is for *you*. It's to improve your

Two views of the hand signal for heel forward. It's a forward motion of your left hand, palm forward, over your dog's head.

timing and effectiveness. The dog will improve in direct proportion to your improvement.

Now that you and your dog both heel well and you are aware from reading previous chapters that your dog must heel whenever he walks (or runs!) on a lead with you, you may be wondering how he will be able to go into the street to urinate or defecate. Simply heel him to the area you have chosen as satisfactory for him to relieve himself, say "Okay," (the release command), followed by something like, "Do your business." Let him have the length of the lead and let him move freely about to urinate and defecate. If he pulls you, give a sharp jerk on the lead, letting it out quickly again. Jerk hard every time he pulls, and he will quickly learn that having six feet of lead doesn't mean he can pull you. When he has finished urinating and defecating, command him to return to heel. Then continue your walk.

You may be interested to learn that an obedience-trained dog never urinates or defecates while under command. So if yours is one of those dogs who try to urinate in every elevator or lobby or on every sidewalk, remember to keep demanding his attention to obedience work so that he hasn't an opportunity to do *anything offensive*. After all, he can't very well lift his leg to urinate on the elevator wall if he's *sitting* at your heel, can he?

Sit-Stay "Stay" is not only a command of obvious convenience but also, in all probability, will save your dog's life more than once. It will enable you to handle him with ease when a child wants to pet him on the street, when the veterinarian needs to examine him on the table, when you desire to groom him, when he is sitting in a store waiting for you to pay for a purchase; in fact, many times every day.

The sit-stay is most easily taught as part of the heeling lessons. Do enough heeling with your dog, before starting the stay work, to make sure he is calmed down, well under control, and attentive. Have him sitting at heel, you with the lead held correctly in your right hand, your left hand hanging at your side, hand over the lead.

Now let go of the lead with your left hand and as you say, "Stay," very firmly, even loudly the first few times, give him

In teaching your dog to sit and stay, let go of the lead with your left hand and as you say, "Stay," very firmly, give him the hand signal: your left hand, palm toward him, moving from directly in front of him up to his face.

the stay hand signal (the left hand, palm toward him, moving from directly in front of him up to his face). This head-on motion *toward* him keeps him from dashing forward; he doesn't want to collide with your hand.

Then you let the lead hang loosely (tension on the lead will make him move forward, following the lead), and you move out in front of him a few feet, facing him, repeating, "Stay," once or twice in a very firm, no-nonsense tone. Walk slowly back and forth in front of the dog, telling him to stay. As he begins to show signs of being reasonably settled, begin to make a half-circle in front of him, then a full circle counterclockwise around him, coming back to stand in front of him, facing him. Then back away from him a little farther

As your dog becomes secure in the sit-stay, move away from him to the end of the six-foot lead and drop it completely.

until you can go to the end of the six-foot lead. Now drop it completely.

If the dog moves while on stay, get back to him *fast*. Using the lead (left hand over it, please), pitch him (yes, his feet actually leave the ground) back to the place he was before he moved. I don't mean *almost* the place, but *exactly* where he was. If he creeps forward even an inch, toss him back with the lead (left hand, again). Make the toss *fast and hard* so that he learns he can't get away with anything. If you make a couple of effective corrections, he won't even try to break his stays in the future.

While your dog is staying, be sure to keep your own awareness level up. You must be prepared to ward off impending disaster *before* it happens. If you see another dog coming, tell yours to stay and move near him so that you can enforce the command before the other dog gets to you. Tell your dog, "Stay!" in a tone that implies instant death if he moves! He won't.

When you return to your staying dog, go to your right, around behind him to heel position, making sure that he doesn't get up and turn around as you walk behind him. (If your tone has been firm enough to make him feel secure, he won't get up.) Once you are back at heel, you can decide

If your dog breaks the sit-stay, get back to him fast and, using your left hand on the lead, pitch him back to his original position before moving.

whether to release your dog from stay (with an "Okay") or do some other command.

He must never be allowed to break his stay before you are back in command. Otherwise, as you return to him in a store after paying for your purchase, he may get up and run off, even out the door. Let him become accustomed to your returning to heel, getting your packages together, your coat buttoned, and so on, then reaching down, picking up his lead, and heeling him off, or whatever.

Once your dog has begun to stay reasonably well while you're at the other end of the lead, start dropping the lead as you leave him after the stay command. And do leave him quickly. If you tell him to stay and then pause, he will believe the matter to be "negotiable" and begin fiddling around down there. So move fast, decisively, away from him, and turn around to face him from a distance.

It is particularly relevant to teach him to stay when the lead is dropped suddenly. Then, on that inevitable day when you drop the groceries, his lead, your gloves, or something else, he will simply sit and stay automatically rather than running off, perhaps across a busy highway. The stay command provides safety only to the degree you can rely on it.

You will also find this command useful in conditioning a shy or nervous dog to accept the attention of friends and eventually strangers. Have the dog sit and stay, and stand at his side, before someone approaches him. Let the visitor approach him slowly (allowing Superdog to sniff the back of his hand), then gently touch the top of his head and pet him softly while talking to him pleasantly. The dog will gain a great deal of confidence this way and eventually have the opportunity to learn that many visitors can be quite nice! Be very sure, though, that no one ever teases or roughs up the dog while he is under the stay command—or at any other time, for that matter.

Getting to Heel Position Once your dog has begun to heel with reasonable responsiveness, you can proceed to a series of steps to give him a good comprehension of the *concept* of where heel is. These heeling steps are an extremely useful exercise in teaching your dog to get his head together. They will also teach you how to maneuver the dog effortlessly. As soon as you've got these steps going, begin using them in your daily routines. You will notice many occasions when, for instance, you are standing with your dog sitting at heel and you suddenly have to move back a pace to let someone else through a doorway. Or you must move to the side in order to let someone walk past you in a narrow passageway.

Giant step forward: With your dog sitting at heel, you loosen the lead and give him a stay command. Then you take a giant step forward, leaving the dog where he is.

Then say, "Heel," and pull him sharply forward to your heel and into a sit. (See chalk diagram.)

There are four basic steps to learn, from which the dog will gather how to move from all the many other points possible. Let's start with the simplest:

1. Have your dog sitting at heel, on your left. Loosen the lead considerably, give the dog a stay command, and take a giant step forward, leaving the dog where he is. Then say "Heel" and pull him sharply forward to your heel and into a sit. Praise him! Repeat this exercise three or four times so

Giant step to right: In starting position for teaching dog to move to his right, he's sitting at heel, on your left.

Then you loosen the lead, give a stay command, and take a giant step to your right, leaving the dog where he is.

Say, "Heel," and pull the dog toward your heel.

that he gets the idea that heel needn't mean a lengthy
walk—but only a step or two into heel position. Then go to
the next stage of our canine Simon Says game.

2. Have your dog sitting at heel, on your left. Loosen the
lead once again, give a stay command, and take a giant step to
your right, leaving the dog where he is. Tell him to "Heel"
pulling him *toward your heel*, turning him sharply forward
to parallel the direction you're facing as he gets to heel. It is
most important that you direct him toward your heel first.
His natural inclination will be to head for your toe, expecting
to sit there and be at heel. Naturally, he wouldn't be at heel,
but rather, a few inches in front of you, looking back over his
shoulder and wondering why he didn't end up at heel. (Since
he doesn't have a driver's license, he doesn't understand that
you have to worry about the rear end of a car when you park
it, not just the front, where your head is.) Repeat this
exercise a few times, making sure you give him the command
before pulling him over to you so that once he gets the idea,
he will have the opportunity to get up and move properly
without being pulled. Remember, the idea is for him to do it
himself, quickly and smartly—not for you to drag him over to

*After pulling dog toward your heel, turn him sharply forward to
parallel the direction you're facing and into a sit at heel. (See chalk
diagram.)*

heel indefinitely. Once he begins to move in the right direction with some certitude, begin to give him a little variety by interchanging this step with the step I just described in (1). Thereafter you can proceed to the next step.

3. Have the dog sitting at heel, on your left again. Loosen the lead several feet. Leaving the dog sitting and staying there, you take a giant step backwards. And though you step backwards, you always face forward. Depending upon the side on which his weight is resting, the dog may naturally turn toward his left or right before heading back toward your heel. The direction at this initial stage does not matter, but as you say "heel" and give him a tug toward you, make sure the U-turn he makes at your heel is from the outer part of the U to the inside, next to you. (Look at the chalk diagram.) If you have difficulty following it, get some chalk and draw the dotted line and arrows on the sidewalk or driveway. It is of the utmost importance that the dog make the final part of the U from outside to inside to end up parallel and close to you, whether the overall form is that of a reverse S or a C. Now, the dog will at first be very confused by this maneuver, so it will seem to you that you need to drag him. Not so at all. When you have initially said "Heel," give a hard jerk on the lead, toward you, immediately letting up. He will move toward you, of course, and slow down, waiting to see what happens next. At this moment slide your left hand down the lead, give another quick jerk on the lead, flipping him into the U-turn and into heel, at a sit. If the lead is loose, your left arm down, relaxed, your left hand properly *over* the lead, you will find it quite simple to flip a dog twice your own weight into this heel position.

Don't waste energy trying to drag him, dead weight, resisting, the whole way. Use the two separate tugs, with the quick flip on the second one. With a bit of practice—in fact, by the time *you* have mastered the "quick flip"—you will find the dog doing the maneuver all by himself. Please note that the dog's *entire body must pass you* and turn around in order for him to end up at heel. If he begins making the U at a point that's even with your toe, he will end up sitting a bit in front of you, once again looking over his shoulder and wondering what went wrong.

Teaching dog to move back: After starting with dog sitting and staying properly at heel, you take a giant step backward. Though you step backward, you always face forward. If the dog's weight is resting toward his right he will turn in that direction and back toward you. Give him a tug toward you, guiding him back toward heel but beyond your foot in a deep U, his body passing you completely and turning forward into the heel position. Be sure that the U at your heel is from the outer part of the U to the inside, next to you. In other words, at the deepest point in the U, turn the dog toward you. (See chalk diagram.)

If your dog is very large, fat (therefore, off-center), or stubborn, you might find one additional bit of information helpful: as you take your left arm back to flip him through the U, move your left foot back also, transferring your weight to the left side. Then your weight will be moving in the same direction you wish his weight to move. In addition, he will follow the left foot. Once your left foot, your weight, and the dog are at the deepest point of the U, bring your left foot forward again, to a point even with your right, and flip the dog through the U into heel position at the same time.

Practice this maneuver without the dog first. Get the left hand and foot moving together. Then try it with the dog. Shifting your weight is the key with a big dog. Just remember, your right foot *never* moves, only your left. After you and Superdog have practiced this step a bit and he has indicated an understanding (which will come about a half of a second after *you* have indicated an understanding), start mixing it with the other two steps (the steps forward and the steps right) learned previously. And compliment your dog as you go. This is a hard one for you, but don't become so tense you forget to tell him how pleased you are. Then go on to the fourth step.

4. This step is known in the formal obedience terms used in Trial work as the Finish. It is part of the Recall (come) exercise and may be performed in any number of ways. I'll teach you the most common way, which is also the easiest and safest and fits most readily into the situations your dog has already grasped.

The dog must be sitting in front of you, facing you, toe to toe, *no more than a few inches away*. Loosen the lead, your left hand over it as usual. Tell the dog to heel, slide your left hand down the lead, give a quick jerk toward your left side, taking him once again through a U with a quick flip as just described in step (3). And here again, you will find it advantageous to use a quick flip instead of a slow drag, to take the dog all the way past you before turning him forward, to move your left foot (and your weight therewith) backwards with him and then forward with him into heel, never moving your right foot.

As soon as you have flipped him around through the U into

Teaching dog to move back (variation): After starting with dog sitting and staying properly at heel, you take a giant step backward. Though you step backward, you always face forward. If the dog's weight is resting toward his left, he will turn in that direction and back toward you. Give him a tug toward you, guiding him back toward heel but beyond your foot in a deep U, his body passing you completely and turning forward into the heel position. Be sure that the U at your heel is from the outer part of the U to the inside, next to you. In other words, at the deepest point in the U, turn the dog toward you. (See chalk diagram.)

a sit at heel, *praise him!* Repeat this exercise a few times; it should be relatively easy if you and he mastered (3), since this one is just another variation. Once he moves readily, mix it up again, doing all four steps in varying sequence.

All four of these steps may be taught to your dog within about ten minutes and to a level of understanding at which he begins to perform them himself—provided you have understood them yourself previously. That's why it's a good idea to practice them first with the lead and without the dog. Or even to draw the patterns on the sidewalk in chalk and walk through them a few times before expecting of Superdog what you cannot yet expect of yourself. Once you've got it straight in your head, you'll realize it's about as easy as dancing.

Once the dog is moving easily to heel and you no longer need your left hand actively on the lead, you should add the hand signal indicating to the dog that he is to move to heel position, or "finish." It is a counter-clockwise circular motion with your left hand, at your left side. As you move your hand in this pattern, you will notice it actually traces the steps your dog takes to "finish." Nothing hard about that.

Down, Sit From Down (Doggy Pushups) "Down" is the command given when you wish your dog to lie down. It is a very important command to the dog owner because down is the position in which the dog is most likely to remain quiet and under control at such times as when visitors are sitting about the living room or you have your dog with you and are visiting someone else.

Down also has particular significance because in the animal world the prone position is submissive, vulnerable. So when a dog downs on command, he is indicating his willingness to accept you as his superior.

But for this very reason, the down command may present great difficulty in the initial teaching phase. The dog may resist downing if he is still resistant to authority in general. An aggressive dog may even become quite nasty about the whole thing. I therefore beg that you take all advice in this chapter quite seriously since it is designed not only to teach the dog the command and establish your authority over him but also to protect you. Read the instructions very carefully. In downing the dog, you will be lowering yourself physically and thereby lowering your authority level at the same time you are challenging him. Proceed with caution. *Keep your face away from the dog!*

If you are working with a small, nonaggressive dog, sit on the floor with him while he has the training collar on. Put him directly in front of you. Take the live ring (the one that moves) of the collar in your left hand, leaving your right hand free. As you say "Down," make a downward sweep with your right hand, palm down, right in front of the dog. Pull down on the collar with your left hand, and at the same time with your right hand push down and *backwards* on the dog's shoulders, repeating, "Down," and making encouraging sounds.

Once he is flat on the floor, keep him there, with tension on the collar if necessary, repeating, "Down," a few times so that he associates the position with the command. Then say,

If your dog is very large, fat (therefore off-center), or stubborn, you may find this maneuver helpful. As you take your left arm back to flip the dog through the U, move your left foot back also, transferring your weight to your left side. As a result, your weight will be moving in the same direction you wish your dog's weight to move. Practice this maneuver first without your dog, making sure you get your left hand and left foot moving together.

"Sit," and at the same time make an upward motion with the right hand, palm up (as previously discussed in the chapter on the sit command), and jerk up on the live ring of the collar with your left hand. The dog will, of course, come up into a sitting position. Praise him! Leave him sitting a moment, then go into the down again.

It is most important that you pull him down with the collar as well as giving the voice and hand command and pushing his shoulders back. Within a few minutes, you will notice that if you give the command and hand signal and pull lightly on the collar, he will go down without being pushed. If, on the other hand, you push him down without using the collar to pull him down (the collar is your authority symbol, remember?), he will assume this is *your* daily workout, rather than a command, and will not respond for some time.

So remember to give the command and hand signal; then a split second later, pull him down, pushing on the shoulders only to whatever degree may be necessary, or not at all. Once he is responding to voice and hand command and a light tug on the collar, you will very shortly notice him downing without the aid of the collar.

Don't be surprised if he sits up from down before he downs from sit, or vice versa. Unfortunately, few dogs do both maneuvers equally well in the same period of time. One step always seems to precede the other, and an owner may conclude the dog understands one and not the other. Nonsense! He understands both but has chosen to do only one.

Just keep practicing. Any dog can be taught within twenty minutes to down well and to sit from down well, with no tug on the lead and nothing more than a verbal and hand command. The only thing standing in your way may be your own timid authority level—so get tough! Or at least sound as if you mean business.

Once the dog is downing nicely in front of you, put him in the heel position, with you standing normally. Bringing your

The finish: With your dog sitting immediately in front of you, no more than a couple of inches away, loosen the lead, your left hand over it as usual. Tell the dog to heel (hand signal for finish, as shown, is a counter-clockwise circular motion with your left hand at your left side) and slide your left hand down the lead toward the collar. Give the dog a quick jerk toward your left side, taking him through a U to heel. You get the dog there by taking him all the way past you before turning him forward, shifting your left foot (and your weight) backwards with him and then forward with him into heel, never moving your right foot.

right hand across in front of him in a downward motion, say "Down." He probably will look at you in confusion or defiance. Repeat the motion and command, and at the same time, lean down and pull down on the collar with your left hand. As he downs, praise him greatly. Then have him sit by giving the voice and hand command (right hand, please, with hand extended and palm up) and pulling him up sharply. Praise again! Repeat this procedure a few times.

If he is still a bit slow to down, you will get tired of bending over him to pull him down, so put your left foot on the lead instead and gently ease him down while repeating the command and hand signal (the left hand may hold the lead as your left foot takes him down, leaving your right hand free for the simultaneous hand signal).

His first reaction may be to fight the foot-on-lead

Chalk diagram on pavement illustrates giant step forward. Handler (H) moves first, and then dog (D) moves to sit at heel. Small interior arrows point in direction handler and dog are looking.

This diagram shows moves in giant step to right. Handler (H) moves first, and then dog (D) moves over to correct position for sit at heel.

Diagram for giant step backward when weight of dog (D) is to his right. Handler (H) moves first, stepping backward but still facing forward. Notice dog's path: a sort of S curve, with final part resembling letter U.

Giant step backward when weight of dog (D) is to his left goes like this. Handler (H) moves first, stepping backward but still facing forward. Notice that dog's path overall resembles a capital letter C, with final part resembling letter U.

The finish. Handler (H) and dog (D) begin in positions facing each other (internal arrows show directions they face). Dog moves through path indicated by chalk marks, going through a U and into a sit at heel.

Teaching dog to lie down. Grasp in your left hand the live ring (the one that moves) of the collar. As you say, "Down," make a downward sweep with your right hand, palm down, directly in front of the dog.

Pull down on the collar's live ring with your left hand, and push down and backwards with your right hand on the dog's shoulders.

Once the dog is lying down, say, "Sit," and at the same time make an upward motion with your right hand, palm up, and jerk up on the live ring of the collar with your left hand.

When your dog is downing nicely in front of you, teach him to down from the sit at heel. Give the down command and hand signal. At the same time, lean down and pull down on the collar with your left hand.

violently. If so, go back to using your left hand to down him until he eases off a bit. Then return to the foot-on-lead method so that you don't have to continue bending over him. If he downs this way but slowly, quicken your foot action. You'll notice he quickens the down! You will promptly notice also that when you give a very firm voice command, accompanied by a hand signal, he will down without the assistance of the lead.

If you are working with a larger, nonaggressive dog, follow the foregoing instructions. But if you find it difficult to push the dog down by putting pressure on his shoulders, pull his front feet forward *gently,* instead. Otherwise, the method is the same.

If you are working with an aggressive dog, a snappy dog, or a snarly dog, the same basic methods apply—but with greater caution and several changes. However, long before you start the actual teaching of the command, make things a little easier for yourself: for some days or even weeks prior to starting down, make sure all your dog's other responses to commands (heel, sit, stay) are working *very well.* In addition, every time you see him about to lie down, say, "Superdog, down!" in a commanding tone.

Yes, this is the coward's way out. But if you make this a practice for some time before beginning formal downing, you will be a lot safer because he will be somewhat accustomed to the idea. And you will also find yourself

Once the dog is down, have him sit by giving him the voice and hand (right hand) commands and pulling him up sharply, again with the left hand.

expending much less effort if your dog is prepared for the whole concept in advance.

This approach is not a joke, as you people with aggressive dogs will learn. Aggression is a deadly serious situation to be avoided and controlled at all costs. The down command is very necessary to this control, but no one needs to get killed teaching it. When you actually begin teaching your aggressive dog to down, *keep your face well away from him*, and work with the dog in the heel position. Your hand on the collar should pull him down very slowly, as should your foot on the lead. In this situation, don't ever look him in the eye or bend down over him with your head approaching his. Simply do everything very slowly and firmly—no arguments, no confrontations. After he has learned to down well at heel, move him in front of you and teach down in that position.

Once your dog has begun to down quickly on voice or hand command alone in front of you and at heel, you will want to teach him to down when at a distance from you (like across the room during a cocktail party). Put him in front of you, sitting and staying, with his lead on. Stand a few feet in front of him, facing him with your right side turned slightly toward him. Take the lead *loosely* in your left hand. With your right hand and voice, give him the down command. If he does not respond immediately, put your right foot on the lead, repeat voice and hand command, simultaneously

If your dog is slow to down from sitting at heel, put your left foot on the lead and gently ease him down while repeating the command and hand signal. Note that left hand holds gathered lead and that right hand is free for the simultaneous hand signal.

pulling him down with your foot. Praise him. Then give him the sit command and hand signal with your right hand, jerking the lead up hard with the left. He'll sit, all right. Repeat the command close in front of him until he is obeying completely.

Then back away a foot or so and repeat the process. Keep backing away until the dog is obeying all the way at the end of the six-foot lead. When he doesn't respond, obviously, you must move (fast!) in nearer again, and work your way back out. But in all probability, his lack of response indicates your authority level is not high enough. Be more commanding in your tone!

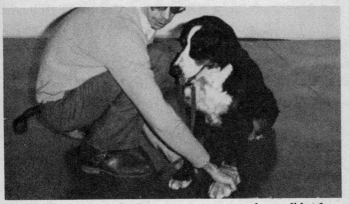

If you are working with a larger, nonaggressive dog, pull his front feet forward gently, while commanding, "Down."

Left: To teach your dog to down at a distance from you, begin by standing in front of him, facing him, with your right side turned slightly toward him. Take the lead loosely in your left hand. Give him the voice and hand commands to down. Put your right foot on the lead, pulling him down with your foot.

Right: With the dog down in front of you, command him to sit and give him the hand signal with your right hand while you jerk the lead up hard with your left.

If obedience is excellent at this point, it will be good at a much greater distance as well. Try it. Try it a lot. The next time you have guests for dinner, have the dog sit about twenty feet from the table. Then when your guests are all seated, give him the down hand signal alone (much more impressive, you know) followed by the stay hand signal. As he lies there calmly, waiting for the command to join the men for after-dinner cigars in the drawing room, dinner-table conversation won't be lacking.

Drop on Heel Here's an exercise that will generally improve your dog's awareness and specifically improve his downs. Among those of us who enjoy obedience trial competition, this exercise is used to prepare a dog for what is known as the drop on recall in "Open" work. It is not in itself, however, part of any ring procedure.

As you are heeling along, get the lead completely into your left hand. Then *without stopping*, suddenly drop to the ground, with your right knee lower, turned across your dog's path. As you do so, yell, "Down!", give the down hand signal in front of his face with your right hand as you drop, and pull him downward with the lead in your left hand.

If this sounds like a lot to do simultaneously in a split second, it is. But all the motions coordinate naturally, as you will see if you try them first without the dog. Get yourself together. Then move fast, yell loudly the first time, and lo and behold, your dog will be flat on the ground. In shock.

After the first few times, you will find that you can give the command in a normal tone of voice, and with a little more practice, you won't have to drop all the way to the ground. Eventually, you won't have to drop at all. He will.

You will find this exercise helps you keep your authority high and teaches your dog to respond to a new command even when moving and concentrating on another.

Down-Stay The down-stay is handled in the same way as the sit-stay, once you have taught your dog to down. I might add, however, that the down-stay is used for greater, long-term control, such as during dinner, when visitors are present, or when you and your dog are visiting someone else's home. Do

Teaching drop on heel: As your dog is heeling along, get the lead completely into your left hand. Without any prior warning, suddenly drop to the ground, with your right knee lower, turned across your dog's path. As you do so, yell, "Down!", give the down hand signal in front of his face with your right hand, and pull him downward with the lead in your left hand.

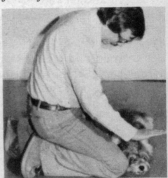

The down-stay is handled the same way as the sit-stay once you have taught your dog to down. Use the same hand signal of the left hand, palm toward him and moving from directly in front of him up to his face.

not make a habit of calling your dog from down. Let it be the time he seems to be glued to the floor.

Recall (Come) Again, let's start with some official words from *Obedience Regulations,* January 1, 1975, Chapter 3, Section 10, p. 23.

"Recall. The principal features of this exercise are that the dog stay where left until called by its handler, and that the dog respond promptly to the handler's command or signal to Come."

"On order from the judge the handler may give command and/or signal to the dog to Stay in the sit position while the handler walks forward about 35 feet to the other end of the ring, where he shall turn and stand in a natural manner facing his dog. On judge's order or signal, the handler will give command or signal for the dog to Come. The dog must come straight in at a brisk pace and sit straight, centered immediately in front of the handler's feet, close enough that the handler could readily touch its head without moving either foot or having to stretch forward. The dog must not touch the handler or sit between his feet."

"On judge's order the handler will give command or signal to Finish and the dog must go smartly to the Heel Position and sit.

Well, those paragraphs are every dog owner's dream. And, with a little effort, they can be reality, too.

First, before you even start this command, make sure Superdog is obeying his other commands well. And—here's the hard part—make sure problems such as housebreaking, destructiveness, and biting have been brought under control. These problems indicate antagonism in the relationship between human and dog. You can hardly expect the dog to come flying in happily, immediately on command, if his feelings about you are somewhat ambivalent.

So sort things out. Get problems under control. Be sure the other obedience commands are working well. And *never* call a dog for any negative reason. If you're angry with him, go get him. If he's out of doors and free, *don't chase after him*. He will then run even further, perhaps into the road. Either sit down and wait for him to come back to you (and don't grab at him when he gets there, but instead offer him a tidbit) or run *away* from him; he'll catch up. But above all, *never* call him and punish him!

So now you've solved all the world's problems and are ready to teach your dog to come. Before actually starting, put a few tidbits of cheese or meat in your pocket.

In teaching recall, have the dog sit and stay at your heel. After you command him to stay, let the lead drop loose, with only your right hand holding the handle. Walk way from the dog as far as you can go without putting any tension on the lead. Turn around and face the dog.

Call him in a crooning tone: "Superdog, come." Pull him sharply toward you, right up squarely in front of you into a sit.

Now have the dog sit and stay at your heel. After commanding him to stay, let the lead drop loose with only your right hand holding the handle. Walk away from the dog as far as you can go without putting *any* tension on the lead. Turn around and face the dog. Just stand there a few seconds. If you call him right away, you will begin to find it impossible to keep him staying, because he will be anticipating the "Come" every time. Having waited those few seconds, you are ready to call him.

However, you don't just *call* the dog. You seduce him. You let him know that getting to you has just got to be the greatest thing that ever happened. (Isn't it?) You do so by calling his name firmly followed by a firm but lilting, two-tone, "Co-ome," the first syllable slightly higher in tone. The effect is something like a two-tone doorbell. No martial command here, please.

All right, back to work. You're standing there and calling your dog in that crooning tone: "Superdog, co-ome!" As you do so, pull him sharply toward you, right up squarely in front of you, accompanied by words and encouragement. Then tell him quickly to sit, pulling up on the lead so that he sits indeed. Praise him lavishly.

With him sitting in front of you, give him the stay command again and back away from him to the end of the loose lead. Wait a few seconds and repeat the command.

With your dog sitting in front of you, give him a stay command again and back away from him to the end of the loose lead.

Make it a happy tone! Make sure he comes in quickly by encouraging him verbally and by using the lead to move him fast.

You will find you handle the lead better in teaching come if you learn to bring it in hand over hand. And as your dog comes scooting in, you must then make sure he sits straight, immediately in front of you. If he tends to go off to one side, bend over as he comes in and straighten out his body with a hand on either side. Do it pleasantly, though, or he'll stop coming.

As your dog indicates his willingness to get up and come to you without your pulling him, start to give him a tiny piece of meat or cheese the instant he sits in front of you. Do this a few times while holding the lead formally. Then have him stay, as usual. Drop the lead, walk away, and call him. In all probability he will come running. *Make sure he sits*, and then give him his reward, with a lot of love.

If he doesn't run to you the first time you drop the lead, go grab the lead quickly and pull him in, pleasantly, and give him his reward. He'll get the idea quickly enough and begin to respond to your commands. As this happens, start adding to the verbal command the come hand signal: extend your right arm directly away from your body and bring your palm in toward your chest in a beckoning motion. Yes, it's exactly the same sign we give to people we wish to have approach us.

As your dog shows his willingness to get up and come to you without your pulling him, reward him with a tiny piece of meat or cheese the instant he sits in front of you.

From then on, you will find that you can leave Superdog staying and move farther away, calling him to you finally and giving him his reward. Thereafter, the greatest fun for him and you can be a good game of Hide 'n' Seek in which you have him sit and stay while you leave the room and hide. You then call him, and he will run to find you, sitting in front of you to receive his reward. You will find that a good deal of the Hide 'n' Seek practice indoors will result in a dog that comes immediately when called outdoors—so long as he knows *before going out* that you have his reward.

You may ask, "But do I have to go through life with a piece of cheese in my pocket in order to be able to rely on my dog's coming back to me?" The answer is no. We use the food reward only to instill a positive reaction to the recall command. After several weeks of positive results, you can begin to taper off on the use of food reward. Give it only every second time, then every third time, and so on. But remember, anytime your dog does not come promptly, anytime you take him somewhere new that has a lot of distractions, anytime he doesn't come directly in and sit, *resume offering the food reward*. Don't try to fight his refusal to come by throwing him around with the lead; you'll end up with a dog who *runs away* when called.

Bear in mind always that your calling Superdog in a pleasant, seductive tone does not mean your voice lacks authority. "Superdog, co-ome," is just as authoritative as any other command, but the manner is different and implies pleasure. After all, what else can possibly bring your dog back to you immediately, on the first command, when he is fifty feet away, off lead, playing with a group of dogs? Only the offer of something better, combined with the tone of authority that makes him *sure* it's better.

If you have read carefully the quotation from the AKC standard at the start of this section, you will notice that the recall exercise is actually made up of three parts: 1) sit and stay, 2) come on command, and 3) finish. The finish is simply the dog's finishing to the heel position from directly in front of you. This command was taught as step (4) in the chapter on steps to heel position.

When you're practicing the recall exercise, *don't* have

your dog finish to heel every time. If you do, he may begin to get up and finish before being told to do so, or he may begin to go directly into the heel position as he comes in instead of sitting in front of you. Either variation is unacceptable. Your dog must come directly in and sit straight in front of you within immediate reach (without your stretching); otherwise, he is likely to run off before you have him under control. When he's sitting properly in front of you, then he may finish to heel when commanded by you.

Remember, your dog hasn't read the rule book. He doesn't know that in formal obedience terms, the recall exercise ends with the finish to heel. So when you're working with him, mix things up a bit. After he has sat in front of you, why not down him, or leave him staying and go off and call him again?

And speaking of formalities, food may be used in teaching recall, but it may *not* be used in the obedience ring at trials. So you should certainly not be dependent upon it in the long term. Nor should you get into the habit of holding your hands in front of you as if you have food. In fact, the obedience regulations specify that your arms must drop loosely and naturally to your sides.

Recall will be most effective when you have made it a routine part of your dog's life, simply calling him whenever you think of it around the house, praising him when he has sat in front of you, occasionally calling him *urgently* when he is busy at play so that he learns to pull himself up short and come to you no matter how enticing the distractions. You must be more enticing!

Stand-Stay Stand-Stay is most often used by the average dog owner when grooming his dog and should be practiced whenever the dog is groomed, as well as during normal obedience sessions. Obviously, the stand-stay is also of great assistance to anyone wishing to examine the dog—the veterinarian or the dog owner wishing to check for ticks.

The AKC obedience regulations describe the stand-stay (Stand for Examination) as follows:

"The handler shall take his dog on leash to a place indicated by the judge, where the handler shall remove the leash and give it to a steward who shall place it on the judge's table or other designated place.

"On judge's order the handler will stand and/or pose his dog off leash by the method of his choice, taking any reasonable time if he chooses to pose the dog as in the show ring. When he is ready, the handler will give his command and/or signal to the dog to stay, walk forward about six feet in front of the dog, turn around and stand facing the dog.

"The judge shall approach the dog from the front, and shall touch only the dog's head, body and hindquarters, using the fingers and palm of one hand only. He shall then order, 'Back to your dog,' whereupon the handler shall walk around behind his dog and return to the Heel Position. The dog must remain standing until after the judge has said 'Exercise finished'."

The regulations also state: "The principal features of this exercise are that the dog stand in position before and during the examination, and that the dog display neither shyness nor resentment."*

You will note that the manner of posing (standing) the dog is optional. I'll give you three different methods and mention the type of dog for whom each is recommended. But obviously, if you get into competition you may use any method you wish.

(1) Toy breeds are usually posed by placing the left hand between the dog's rear legs and the right hand under the chest between the front legs, spreading the fingers of each sufficiently to set the legs out squarely, saying "Stay," firmly, as you do so. Once the dog is set up, remove the right hand, saying, "Stay," again as you do so and giving the stay hand signal with the right hand. Then place the right hand on the rear quarters of the dog, pushing *gently* downward while holding the rear end up at the same time with the left hand—do all this as if you were examining the dog; do it very seriously; no friendly, funny remarks to the dog in the process. You will note that the dog soon realizes he may not sit down. Then slowly remove your left hand (but keep it nearby), repeating, "Stay." At first, you will not be able to leave the dog for more than a few seconds, without his

*Obedience Regulations, January 1, 1975, Chapter 3, Section 7, p. 22-3.

Toy breeds are usually posed by placing the left hand between the dog's rear legs and the right hand under the chest between the front legs. As you do so, you spread the fingers of each hand enough to set the legs out squarely and you say, "Stay," firmly.

When the dog is set up reliably, give him the stay command and walk away from him to a place about six feet in front of him.

After you have walked away from your dog and are standing about six feet away and facing him, have a friend walk over and touch him on the head, shoulders, and hindquarters, making no conversation and then walk away.

walking off or sitting. But keep at it. Never permit your dog to sit directly from the stand-stay.

As his stand-stay becomes more reliable and willing, set him up by simply leaning down, putting hands under either end as usual; tell him to stay while giving him the stay hand signal. Walk away from him to a place about six feet in front of him; turn to face him; stand there awhile and have a friend or relative work over and touch him on the head, shoulders, and hind quarters, *making no conversation*, and walk away.

The first time this is done, stand ready to return to the dog quickly and set him up again if he moves when approached by the other person. You may, in fact, have to hold a hand under him a few times while someone "examines" him until he gains some confidence. After the person who has examined him walks off a few feet, return to your dog by going to the right, behind him, around to the heel position. Stand there a few seconds; then heel him forward a few paces and go into another command or release him with much praise. Again, don't let him sit from stand or you will find that he sits automatically every time you return to him—or when you are right in the middle of grooming him.

(2) With a medium-to-large dog, posing is somewhat simpler. You don't have to bend over to set him up. Instead, as you are heeling him along, reach out with your left hand and place it on his right thigh where it curves into the

Posing a medium-to-large dog: As your dog is heeling along (whether on lead or—as here—off), reach out with your left hand and place it on his right thigh where it curves into the stomach. Just place your hand there lightly as you stop walking and say, "Stay." Your hand, properly placed, will prevent your dog from sitting, as he should otherwise do.

stomach. Just place it there lightly, as you stop walking, and say, "Stay." You will find that your hand placed properly will prevent him from sitting. Stay with him, keeping your left hand there as you bring your right hand over to examine him and put a little pressure on his hind quarters, while holding him up with your left hand and repeating, "Stay." He will quickly realize that he is to stay, not to sit. When he is calm and standing, give him another stay command and walk off, six feet away from him, and have someone examine him as just described in (1). Return to him in the recommended way.

(3) The large breeds, and occasionally the medium and smaller ones, may be taught to stand and stay by heeling with them normally; then as you're moving at a moderate pace (not fast), give a stay signal with your left hand accompanied by a *sharp* voice command to Stay. Stop with the dog yourself the first few times; if he tends to sit, use the method just described in (2). If not, simply repeat the stay command and move off so that he may be examined by your friend.

You will find quite quickly that the catch to this method is *your* timing. If you actually stop *before* giving the stay command, the dog will of course start to sit. After all, that's what you've been teaching him for weeks. So don't blow up at him. Straighten out your own timing and he will have no problems.

When your dog is calm and standing, give him the stay command and walk off six feet from him and turn so that you face him. Have someone examine him— touching head, shoulders, and hindquarters.

Return to your dog by going past him to your right and then around behind him in a U to end up in the correct position for heel.

The large breeds may be taught to stand and stay by starting with the dog heeling along normally. While you're moving at a moderate pace, give a stay signal with your left hand and simultaneously a sharp voice command to stay.

For the shy, nervous, or aggressive dog, the stand for examination is the ultimate command. A dog who will let you decide who may examine him and will stand quietly to be gone over by a stranger—whether he likes it or not—is a dog who has recognized his pack leader and put himself in his hands.

TWO DOGS—THE OBEDIENCE BRACE

If you have two dogs (or more), you may wonder how to walk them together and in general, how to train them in relation to one another.

First of all, they must be trained *very well* individually. Then you secure a coupler, the device that joins the two collars and allows you to use one lead for two dogs. Note that in fastening a coupler between the dogs, you must reverse the collar of the dog who will be on the inside (closer to you) so that the collar opens off the coupler instead of on your side.

A coupler, the device that joins two training collars and allows you to use one lead for two dogs.

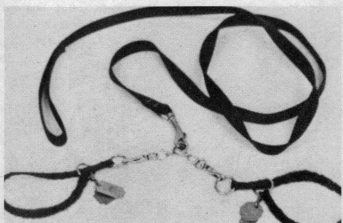

Here's how to rig the six-foot lead, the coupler, and two training collars (taping tags together would cut noise) so that you can walk two dogs about as easily as one. Note that you must reverse the collar of the dog who will be on the inside (next to you) so that his collar opens off the coupler rather than on your side.

And who is to go on the inside? The smaller dog. If the dogs are the same size, put the more active, pushy dog on the inside. He will do better between you and the steadier dog. The positioning of the dogs, once stabilized, is permanent—not to be changed.

Don't be concerned about correcting the dog who doesn't need correction simultaneously with the dog who does. If you notice, you will see that the proper lead correction will apply force principally to the dog who's out of line.

You will find all commands and handling for both dogs the same as for one dog except that when you begin working with your "obedience brace," *you* will have to learn to control the lead properly on about-turns so that the dogs do not become entangled or cross over one another. You will find it easy to handle the lead on these U-turns if you remember to swing your left arm out and bring the dogs around in a sweeping motion. If you do it properly the first few times, the dogs will take over and manage it themselves thereafter.

You will find great delight in your "brace." Their teamwork and their own pleasure in this coordinated action will be apparent to you, to say nothing of spectators. You will

Left: If you walk two dogs of different sizes, the smaller dog goes on the inside. If dogs are of equal size, put the more active, pushy dog on the inside. The positioning of the dogs is permanent.

Right: A brace heels exactly as does an individual dog.

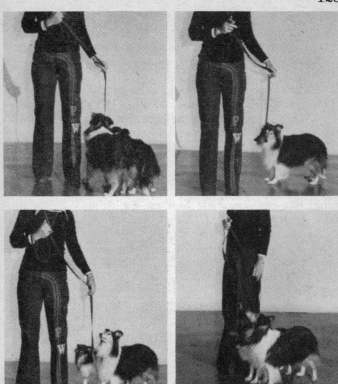

A brace finishes exactly as does an individual dog but will require a bit more space in which to make the U turn.

A brace downs and stays as does an individual dog.

A brace sits and stays and comes on command as does an individual dog.

also notice that the individual work of both dogs will improve when reinforced by "brace" work.

So start scouring the premium lists of dogs shows and the match show notices for "brace" competition. A few trophies would do great things for your mantel!

OFF-LEAD OBEDIENCE WORK

It is of course your goal to have a dog who obeys commands around the house and in the yard without your having a lead on him or having to work through many commands in order to bring him under control. But off-lead work comes slowly—first indoors, then out.

Before you even begin thinking of off-lead work, it is of the utmost importance that the dog behave very well *on* lead. In this connection, learn to control your dog's heeling with only your right hand on the lead. Drop your left hand completely. This procedure will force you to improve both your timing and the authority expressed by your verbal commands.

Once you're controlling your dog's heeling with only your right hand on the lead, you should progress to heeling and all other commands with your dog's lead dragging on the floor where you can grab it if necessary to correct him, but where he realizes you're not holding it. Anytime your dog seems confused or unresponsive, pick up the lead quickly and correct him with it—not in a fit of temper, but with a display of authority.

When your dog has become completely responsive with the lead dragging, you will find you can work on stays, down, and recall without the lead—but with the collar on, please. Don't forget to use a food reward on recall occasionally to keep your dog responding at a high level.

Off-lead problems are most apt to appear in heeling. Work first, on the steps to heel position. These will get him moving with you. If he displays confusion or slowness to react, correct him with the collar immediately and firmly. With progress in this area, move on to heeling him forward a few steps at a time, gradually lengthening the distance. If you are fantastically lucky, your dog will heel off-lead quite well. If you and he are normal, though, he will wander from heel. He may lag, forge ahead, or dash off. He is indicating that he has become dependent upon the lead rather than responsive to your authority and willing to follow your commands.

You can get through this stage by buying some fishing line made of nylon monofilament (of whatever weight necessary for your dog) and attaching it to his collar for off-lead practice. Be sure to wrap the line around your right hand several times, as single-strand fish line can cut your flesh badly. I don't wear gloves, but some people do. Now you have a way of controlling him *when necessary*.

Don't use the fish line for anything other than to prevent his running off or lagging far behind. Leave it quite slack between you and the collar so you do not pull on the collar inadvertently. Forging should be corrected with the fast about-turns, remember? Fortunately, you will not be able to overuse the fish line easily because it is quite awkward. However, since the fish line is light in weight, transparent, and odorless, your dog will be only slightly aware of it and certainly won't become dependent upon it.

But he must be dependent upon your commands, the amount of authority you express, and the performance you demand. Off-lead work requires more of you; your dog must rely on your movements, your verbal commands and hand signals, your sureness as you work. Don't let him down.

10
The Problems You Thought He'd Outgrow

THE DOG WHO IS GENERALLY HOUSEBROKEN, BUT . . .

Please start by reading again the sections on diet and housebreaking and by getting prepared to begin obedience training.

Usually poor housebreaking habits in a dog who knows where he is supposed to urinate and defecate indicate a lack of structure and a number of slipups by you—incorrect diet, wrong feeding time, lack of motivation, lack of reasonable walking schedule, and a number of other rather odd quirks of fate. Here's a checklist of corrections:

1. Diet: Put your dog on the correct diet, amount of food, and feeding time immediately. Nothing will work until you straighten out these details.

2. Give him a small liverwurst or cheese reward every time he urinates or defecates outside.

3. Provide your dog a *small* den in which to stay when you are out.

4. If he (obviously, not she) lifts his leg to urinate on furniture in the house, be sure he is neutered promptly and do not permit him to leg-lift more

than twice on each walk. Leg-lifting simply becomes a habit, but nevertheless, unnecessary. Check out the housebreaking instructions, and be sure to follow those on housebreaking necessities vs. leg-lifting.

5. Make sure your dog defecates outdoors when he should. Use suppositories whenever necessary.

6. If you have cats and litter boxes in the house, put the litter someplace where the dog can't reach it, or get one of those covered litter pans the dog can't get into. Most dogs love to eat dehydrated cat feces from the litter; the result is much water-drinking, much urinating, and much defecating. And much owner disgust the day you walk in and see this feast taking place.

7. When the dog defecates or urinates unexpectedly and unexplainably, check to see whether children or guests fed him some treats the *previous* day. If he urinates unusually for more than one day, call your veterinarian.

8. If you have more than one dog and don't know which one is defecating in the house (of course, you *think* you know, but let's be sure), put a few drops of *green* food coloring in one dog's food every day. Green works best and will show up within twenty-four hours in the dog's stool. Don't discontinue the food coloring until housebreaking has been perfect for several weeks. You never know who might slip up. If you have many dogs, use green food coloring for one, red for another, a different brand of kibble for a third, and the basic kibble for the fourth. If you have more than four dogs, well, just use your imagination.

9. In hot humid weather, dogs frequently drink a great deal of water and have "accidents" if not walked frequently. This problem may be alleviated by providing your dog ice water to drink and ice cubes to eat. Also, you can keep him cool by

spraying him occasionally with cold water. A plastic plant-misting bottle is a convenient way to do it.

10. Following the principles of the instructions in the housebreaking section, keep a lead on your dog at all times when you are home and keep him in the room with you in any way you can—by closing the door, tying him to your chair, tying him to your bed at night, and so on. Be particularly careful to keep him in check while you're on the phone, watching television, or making love. After his obedience work has reached a level of "cooperation," begin letting him be without the lead, but *always* in sight. As the obedience progresses and he indicates his willingness to assume responsibility (work off lead, for example), he will take the same responsibility for his housebreaking.

Anytime he slips, work on the obedience even harder, and keep his lead on whenever you are home. Also, remember the food rewards in the street. Most importantly, regard housebreaking slipups as either "incidents" (deliberate disrespect to be settled by better obedience work) or "accidents" (your fault, to be straightened out by a little more attention).

If your dog is one of those who are a bit sloppy about where they defecate, a little on the sidewalk, a little off, give him a suppository, take him completely into the street and keep him there marching to and fro until he defecates. Then reward him with his bit of liverwurst and praise him wildly. Do this as many times as necessary to insure that he will defecate out in the street, as desired.

Or if he is basically housebroken but slow to perform his toilet acts in the street, or slow just when it rains or snows or whatever, put him on the reward system: a tiny piece of liverwurst or cheese each time he urinates and defecates. And do use suppositories when necessary. It's much better than walking or standing around for long periods while he "thinks about it."

If you have read all this and are sitting there muttering to yourself that all this is very well for everyone else's problem, but you happen to have to dog (or cat) that urinates or defecates in the bathtub—and what do you do about that?—how about getting a cheap plastic shower curtain, hanging it from the shower-curtain rod so that it falls *outside* the tub, and taping it to the tub and walls at the end so the pet can't get into the tub? And do follow the rest of the housebreaking instructions.

EXCITEMENT URINATION

Some dogs, adults and puppies, urinate uncontrollably when a new person comes into the room, when you bend down to pet them, when you chastise them, and so forth. Owners usually describe this as urinating when "excited."

Actually, this is not a housebreaking problem in any sense except when you have to clean up. The dog does not even know he is urinating and should *never, never* be punished for doing so under these circumstances.

This is truly submissive urination, as described in the section on eye contact. And the only way to stop it—gradually, not instantly, unfortunately—is to eliminate the cause, the eye contact, and perhaps other behavior on your part that the dog has come to associate with eye contact and reacts to by urinating.

Start obedience training so as to give your dog more confidence and a greater sense of security. At the same time, stop making eye contact with the dog upon entering the house after an absence. Look over the dog's head. Don't greet him. Just mutter, "Did you have a good day?" or some other inanity. And keep going, or take him out, or whatever, but don't look him in the eye! Try to avoid bending over him. If you must do so, first issue a command, such as "Sit" and "Stay", and keep his attention on that command by repeating it demandingly and with mild encouragement while you bend down to attach his lead.

Make sure that guests don't greet the dog when entering your house. Instead, they should sit down normally and when he comes over to them, talk to him quietly, with little enthusiasm, *without looking him in the eye*. After he has calmed down, they may pet him discreetly when he approaches them. At this stage, they are not to approach him.

As for the submissive urination encountered when you punish your dog, first, get your own head together and stop creating situations in which he must make mistakes and thereafter be punished. Make his life positive, quickly, and this form of urination will disappear overnight. But when you must punish, use the lead and collar as outlined in the chapter on punishment. That kind of punishment will not bring on submissive urination. However, the answer is to vow to do better—*you,* that is.

THE PAPER-TRAINED DOG WHO
CAN'T FIND THE PAPER

We all know of course that the paper-trained dog who can't find the paper is perfectly aware of the location of the paper, since he manages to reach it occasionally, sometimes even frequently. But . . .

Please read again the sections on diet, health, paper-training, and punishment. You will probably find that your problems will be solved after you correct your dog's diet, start rewarding him for using the paper, get the obedience training in hand, and keep a lead on him when you're home—keep him in sight at all times!—until you can get the responsibility onto his back by means of the obedience work. If he has a favorite spot for mistakes ("incidents," right?), block it off with furniture or close the door to that room. Make it hard for him to make mistakes.

But please make sure his paper is readily available to him, and make sure you change the paper every time he uses it—as soon as you have given him his reward. Get into the "clean" habit.

THE 15-FOOT COUCH THAT
DISAPPEARED

Chewing Problems

The prospective client on the other end of the line had just finished telling me how her seven-month-old Weimaraner had totalled a 15-foot, $1,500 couch in half a day. I sat there wondering why anybody would leave a chewer with a $1,500 couch. But then I'm always wondering about such "minor" questions to which the answers seem so obvious, to me at any rate.

Most dogs that chew—"destroy" if you will—are hyperactive. Their needs for discipline and structure have not been met, nor have their needs for exercise and diet. You must take care of all of these needs immediately. Neutering will certainly help. The sooner it's done, the sooner the behavior will change, so have it done now. And proceed to the rest of the instructions while you wait for assistance from the neutering. It does take several weeks for the hormones to work out of the dog's system and allow him to calm down.

His diet should be *dry* kibble (see Diet chapter), a brand that comes in large chunks, fed just before you leave him. If he is hyperactive, don't forget that his food allowance should contain a good proportion of pasta. If he has a penchant for plaster, get some Dolomite tablets at the health food store and add them to his food. Also, leave him some chew bones, preferably the white ones made of beef hide.

But most important, leave him in his den (bath or kitchen stripped of everything he can reach), and leave him *exhausted*. At first, until he becomes accustomed to his den and also calms down a bit, exercise him and do enough obedience to leave him totally exhausted. The obedience commands most useful are the steps to heel position and down/sit/down ("doggy pushups").

Expect to spend at least forty minutes working with him on obedience alone before you leave him. Be extraordinarily demanding of him in his obedience work. Then just leave him in his den with his food, water, and beef-hide chew bones and *go*. Whether or not he goes after the door of his den depends upon how effectively you have worked with him. (To protect your door during this period, you might put up an aluminum or plexiglass kick plate, available at most hardware stores.)

If you do your job well, your dog will be delighted to eat and sleep. If you don't he'll probably scratch at the door for a while. If he does, leave his collar on, leave home normally but wait and go back in, throwing the door open and berating him loudly and firmly. Take the live (moving) ring on the collar, jerk it hard a couple of times, put him through a few more "doggy pushups," give one last *hard* jerk on the collar, and leave again. Repeat this procedure as often as necessary to stop the scratching. "As often as necessary" may be ten times the first occasion, but the necessity will decrease.

Above all, let your dog's scratching or chewing be an indication to you that you must work him harder—and perhaps longer. And then just *do it!* It only takes a couple of days of such work to accomplish the goal; it's not forever if you keep working on his obedience daily so as to fill his needs for structure and discipline in general.

Every once in a while after many weeks of good behavior, a formerly destructive dog will suddenly seem to go berserk and tear apart everything in sight. If you should have this experience, look to the dog's environment, not the dog. Something drastic must have happened to set him off while you were out. It is of course possible that you simply didn't work with him effectively before you left. But obviously you will know that before you go and will be aware of the chance you are taking. But if that's definitely not the reason, you'll generally find that the cause is some very disturbing noise, such as an ugly fight between neighbors, repeated ringing of the door bell, or perhaps even constant ringing of the phone. It could even be a hammer or buzz saw in a neighboring home or apartment that goes on and on. (It would get on your nerves too if you were home!)

Before punishing your dog, please investigate the cause! If the door bell is the culprit, put a cutoff switch on it—and

cut it off as you leave. The telephone company will be
delighted to put an on-off switch on your phones (at a "slight
additional cost" naturally). Seriously, it's worth it to you and
to the dog. It gives him a chance of retaining his sanity.
Anybody who dials your number still hears the usual ringing
sound.

The significant point here, in case you've missed it, is that
the dog will not suddenly go out of his mind. Something in
his environment has to give him a good shove.

In any case, go ahead and order the new couch. Your dog is
not going to be sitting on it while you're gone anyhow. It
won't fit in the bathroom.

THE DOG WHO JUMPS
ON PEOPLE

You may walk through the door each evening dreaming of
an extra-dry martini in front of the television set. But what
your dog has in mind is washing every inch of your face and
perhaps knocking you off your feet in the process. With a
little luck, you can avoid this overpowering welcome by
walking right past the dog, muttering a lukewarm greeting,
instead of confronting him with a gooey hello—which turns
to rage as you pick yourself up from the rug. But most dogs
are so glad to see you—and visitors—that they just must get
to your eye level, where all the attention is.

There is, fortunately, a very simple and pleasant way in
which to stop your dog from jumping on you. As he jumps
up, grab his front feet, one in each of your hands, and hold on
to them. Keep holding, talking to your dog agreeably. Don't
let go. Don't bend over; don't squeeze his paws. Just hold
on, talking all the while as if nothing special were happening.

If he tries to gnaw on your hands, move them back on
either side of you, alongside your hips, but keep holding on.
In fact, hold on until he is in a state of panic over no longer
having four feet to call his own. Then let go and walk away.
Repeat this procedure and instruct everyone who comes in
the door to do the same. Within a few days, you'll notice that

If your dog jumps on you, grab his front feet, one in each hand, and hold on to them. Keep holding as you talk to him agreeably. Don't let him go until he is in a state of panic over no longer having four feet to call his own.

when your dog starts to jump up, he immediately gets a very knowing look on his face and puts his front feet right back down on the floor. Then he will stop jumping up altogether.

Obviously, it's important that everyone in the house assist on this project. Otherwise your dog will learn that there are some people he can jump on and those he can't. If some member of the family—because of age or disability—cannot do his part, or if you expect visitors whom you do not know well enough to include in this "game," get the dog's lead on *before* the confrontation arises. Keep him under control, sitting, that is, until everyone has arrived and settled in. Then he may greet them. He is a social animal, you know!

THE MASCOT OF THE MOVING INDUSTRY

The Dog Who Barks When Left Alone

If you're sitting there eviction notice in hand, take a deep breath and relax. Help is at hand.

The barking dog—that mascot of the moving industry—is most often hyperactive, insecure, and rather spoiled. He also is generally easily upset by strange noises around his home. And since he is insecure, he continues to worry and bark long after the noise has stopped.

So find him a den as far as possible from the front door, elevator shaft, stairway, or whatever else carries commotion. Also, if your dog is jittery, please have him neutered to begin with and start his "denning" as soon as he returns home, since he will have been confined at the veterinarian's office anyway and may be somewhat accustomed to it.

Work with him on obedience as well as general exercise for at least 40 minutes before you leave him, and make sure he is *exhausted*. The steps to heel position and "doggy pushups" work best for this purpose. Be demanding! When you go out, please plan to have several hours available the first day to devote to his correction. Leave your *tired* dog in his den with his food (if he's hyperactive, do mix pasta with his dry kibble, according to instructions in the Diet chapter) and water, beef hide chew bones, and so on, and with the collar on. Go out, lock the door as you normally would, and walk away as usual. But then go off and sit down and wait. Give him time to eat. And see whether he's going to bark. If you hear anything major (don't count a little whining unless it escalates to full-scale "singing"), rush back in throwing the door open and screaming at him. Take his collar by the live (moving) ring, and jerk on it hard while berating him. If necessary, hold the collar tight until he is a little breathless. I say "if necessary" because uncontrolled barking is often the canine equivalent of human hysteria. Tightening the collar for a few seconds to force him to calm down is the equivalent of slapping a hysterical person on the cheek to bring him to his senses. But use your dog's collar; don't slap him!

When you have jerked on the collar to the point where he would rather have you leave, just drop him (and the entire subject) and leave once again, walking off as if you were leaving the building. But go sit down again and wait.

If he starts barking again, go back and repeat the routine. Be prepared to return again and again until he stops barking. You may have to repeat this routine for many hours at first. And even after he has gotten the message and begun to calm down, you must work hard every morning before you leave him and be prepared to wait awhile, and if he barks go back and correct him several times. The situation is one that improves gradually, usually over several days or as much as two weeks. Expect him to bark initially each morning for a week or two, to be corrected once or twice and then to be quiet for the rest of the day.

If you do indeed have an eviction threat, as many clients do when they call our office, tell your neighbors that you have started training and that you would appreciate their cooperation and patience. They should be prepared for some barking over the period of a couple of weeks and should also be kind enough to let you know exactly when the dog barks if they hear him. (And if you get reports he was barking at 2 A.M. on a night you were home, you will know it's not *your* dog that's the problem.)

It is important to you to know whether your dog barks while you are gone, and if so, when and for how long. For instance, it is normal for most dogs to bark in apartment buildings when the hall near their apartment is being vacuumed. They will also bark at first when they hear people going in and out of neighboring apartments. But this will stop shortly. Make sure you have no annoying neighbors who deliberately ring your bell or talk to the dog through the wall. That's not fair!

In one case that proved quite instructive, the client knew her dog was barking and began training to correct the situation. The dog progressed nicely and never barked when she left in the morning, nor did he bark during short periods when he was boarded.

Yet an irascible neighbor complained that the dog barked every morning an hour after my client left for work. In order to check out the truth of the complaint, I had the client telephone me before she left each day and leave her phone off the hook, as I did mine. Then I listened every few minutes. No, the dog did not bark as she left or shortly thereafter. Yes, he did begin barking an hour after she left—but only after I heard someone come to the door of her apartment scratch on it, and call the dog's name. Naturally, the dog went wild!

It turned out—in court—that the neighbor wanted the client's apartment for his daughter, and the apartment scene in New York being what it is, the only way to get it was to complain of her dog—and make sure the dog kept barking!

A more amusing instance arose recently when a client called to advise that the young woman who had just moved in next door was complaining that the dog barked during the day. Now, my colleagues and I all knew the dog to be an older, very quiet, well-behaved pet, and there had been no complaints from the previous tenants. Very strange.

I asked my client to inquire a little more about the circumstances, and particularly to ask other neighbors what they knew. Fortunately, the building was full of busybodies, and the truth came out. The new tenant was a call girl; the dog was barking at the constant ringing of her doorbell and the traffic in and out of her apartment.

I suggested to the client that the dog would, with a little time, become accustomed to the new sounds and that she should advise her complaining neighbor that she would just have to tolerate the barking a bit longer, since "prostitution" is a more serious charge than "barking dog."

THE WHINY BRAT

If there's anything I can't stand, its a whiny dog. Which reminds me of Oscar. His owner commented, as we set out for an obedience trial in Baltimore at 3 A.M.: "He'll quiet down once we get out of Manhattan and pick up some speed."

Some speed? It turned out Oscar didn't calm down until we reached 83 miles an hour—no, not 82 . . . 83! At which point he was lulled into a stupor by the blur of objects flying past the window and hardly whined at all.

Of course, if some six years earlier, every time he started "singing" someone had told him to do something constructive, like sit, and then complimented him, telling him to stay, we might never have progressed to the 83-mile-an-hour game.

If you have a really whiny dog—actually an insecure, unhappy dog—you'll find you must keep his lead on during whatever circumstances bring on the whining, be it at home, in the car, or elsewhere.

The minute he starts, give a *hard* jerk on the lead

accompanied by a command, such as sit, followed by praise, of course. The dog will sit simply because he must and will stop whining momentarily. And then of course, he'll probably begin to rise and start talking again.

Hit that lead again hard, say, "No!" through clenched teeth (the same teeth you have been grinding at the sound of his whining), and repeat the command. Enforce it *toughly* this time and congratulate your dog upon completion of his orders. Let him worry about how far he might have pushed you. And while he's worrying, and carrying out commands and collecting praise, he'll forget about whining.

While he's forgetting to whine, keep him busy with another command. How about down and stay? Keep your performance up at such pace that he simply can't backslide into a whine. And never under any circumstances let a whine escalate to a crescendo before stopping it. He won't get laryngitis at that point (unfortunately), but you will.

THE WAR WITH MA BELL

Barking at Telephones and Doorbells

It almost seems as though our dogs and the telephone company are at war. In our telephone-oriented society, a dog soon learns that the ringing of the phone means his master's attention will be on the call, not on him. Many dogs have taken to barking at the phone, ripping the phone from the wall, or biting people as they go to answer the phone. In one case, a client reported her Giant Schnauzer (weighing in at 110 lbs.) mounted her housekeeper every time she answered the phone. The family had a new housekeeper every week until they decided it might be more appropriate to train the dog.

Obviously, the answer in the longer term is to be able to command your dog to do something other than bark at the phone. So lay the foundation by working on obedience training. In the meantime, however, put your dog's lead and collar on whenever you are home. When the phone rings and he dashes at it or at you, barking, grab the end of the lead and forcefully say, "Sit!", pulling up hard on the lead so as to enforce the command. This action will usually stop the barking. If it doesn't, jerk on the lead even harder and introduce your dog to that old saw, "Shut up!" Every dog should learn it at an early age anyway.

The same principle applies to the dog who barks inordinately at the ringing of the door bell. It's normal for a dog to bark, either from protectiveness or from delight, at a potential visitor when the bell sounds. But enough is enough! After the first few barks, tell the dog, "Thank you for telling me there's someone at the door; now sit and be quiet." Enforce the command with the lead and collar, following the order with praise as you open the door and greet your visitor.

TAKE THE MONEY AND RUN

The Dog Who Grabs Things and Runs Off

Don't be like one client of mine who didn't take the dog's clowning seriously until he swallowed a $100 bill.

The day your dog grabs a glove and plays hide 'n' seek with you, get busy. Dogs grab things and run in order to get attention and discipline. If a dog is getting enough structure, he won't behave this way.

To stop such behavior, do several things:

1. Temporarily eliminate the temptations. Put gloves, magazines, papers, scarves, socks, money, and other small goodies away. Get neat. At least for a couple of months.

2. Start doing some effective obedience work at the *beginning* of each day so that the day begins on the right tone. If the dog grows restless as the day progresses, try a little more work.

3. Be sure the dog always has chewies and dog toys in abundance. (And be sure he doesn't have worms.) Otherwise, your possessions are fair game.

11
The Problems Your Dog Added

THE WHEEL WASN'T INVENTED BY A DOG

Dogs that Chase Cars, Bikes, Children, and So On

It is natural for all dogs, particularly the herding breeds (including German Shepherds and Collies) and the Terriers to chase anything that moves—and to stop it as best they can.

But, obviously, dogs should not be chasing cars. Cars kill. The only answer that truly, reliably works is not to permit your dog to be in circumstances where he could chase a car. In other words, he is not to be out running around alone, unattached, unsupervised. In most communities, such running around loose is against the law anyway.

Chasing bikes and children can be more of a problem, since these temptations are often right in the dog's own yard or living room. To begin the control of this problem, put the dog's training lead and collar on him and leave them on when you are home. Whenever the dog starts to chase, grab the end of the lead, jerk *hard,* and yell, "No!" Then tell the dog to do something positive like "Sit," and praise him. In other words, turn the situation around. Get it under control, and make it positive.

Even more important: Work on getting him under control

before he begins the chase. It will take a bit of practice for you to raise you own awareness level *higher than his*. But that's what you must do.

This change in you should begin to take place, however, as you improve your side of the obedience work. Then instead of having to grab the lead, you can simply give the dog an alternative. When the child starts to run, tell the dog to "Come" and then "Heel" or "Down" or something else useful. And then praise him! You will have succeeded in distracting him as well as controlling him.

Do note that the *obedience* is the real answer, not the lead. When the obedience is effective, you can remove the lead and rely on your voice.

AGGRESSION

This chapter has no funny title, no amusing stories, because aggression is not funny. Pain is not amusing. Scars are forever.

Aggression appears in many forms, any of which is cause for concern. And many forms of aggression are absolutely terrifying. Before dealing with the ways of controlling aggression, it seems worthwhile to describe the signs of aggression and the course the dog's behavior will take if left unchecked.

Many clients complain of their male dogs beginning to growl at other males sometime after six months of age. This form of challenge will, as hormone activity rises, lead to an attempt to dominate, and it will finally escalate to out-and-out attack.

Other dogs show mild aggression toward people by growling slightly, curling their lips, snapping, nipping. Generally these dogs have had to grow up with insufficient structure. That lack has actually been evident in other behavioral problems such as destructiveness, barking, and leg-lifting in the house.

If the owner had dealt with the earlier problem, the aggression probably never would have surfaced. Now, with increased maleness (females rarely show indiscriminate aggression toward people), the dog becomes more and more aggressive, until he usually bites someone severely. This is something like the situation in which a child of eleven steals a pen from the dime store, is caught, and the parents say, "Oh, it's a normal part of growing up. He won't do it again." Then at seventeen, he's arrested for stealing a car and the parents "can't understand how it happened." These trends are predictable, whether in people or animals.

Before reading another word of this chapter, please read again the sections on Sex and the Single Dog, Eye Contact, Protectiveness. They are of utmost importance.

Now that you have read those recommended sections, you can begin to understand the difference between protectiveness and aggression. You also have realized that before anything can be accomplished to correct an aggression problem, your dog must be neutered. (No, frontal lobotomies for dogs aren't recommended.) Have the neutering done *immediately*. Every day you wait constitutes taking an irrational chance.

Aggression Toward People If you are dealing with your dog's aggression toward people, take stock while your dog is at the veterinarian's being neutered. Make a list of the circumstances in which he has shown aggression by growling, showing his teeth, snapping, barking aggressively, nipping, or biting. You will find upon careful observation that these circumstances have certain points in common. Principally: 1) the dog felt threatened; and 2) you had no way to control him without getting hurt.

These conditions must be eliminated *fast*, at the same time you start to make the *permanent* changes to eliminate your helplessness and your dog's fear. Obedience training will accomplish your objectives most effectively. But you will need some additional assistance while you get the obedience training going and then carry it to the level necessary to prevent aggression—and that standard is "trial"level competence within six weeks of the time your dog is neutered, the most critical time of the rest of his life.

The first facet of this "additional assistance" is to keep your dog's lead on *at all times when anyone (including yourself) is in the house*. Everyone must participate in the obedience training and be willing to exercise control over the dog. The purpose of keeping the lead on is to remind the dog through this authority symbol that you are master and also to give you a way of controlling the dog *without getting near him*. In other words, if you need to move him from area to area, to start training, to get him off a piece of furniture to punish him, to groom him, whatever, use the lead and *don't pick it up near the collar*. Pick up the end of it six feet away from him. And pray that he is not as resourceful as my friend Cuddles, the Poodle who crawls under the bed and pulls the lead in after him.

DON'T MAKE ANY OF THE FOLLOWING TEN MISTAKES:

1. DON'T REACH UNDER A PIECE OF FUR-NITURE AFTER THE DOG.

2. DON'T CORNER HIM.

3. DON'T THREATEN TO HIT HIM WITH ANYTHING OR THREATEN HIM WITH YOUR TONE OF VOICE OR EYES.

4. DON'T PUT YOUR FACE UP TO HIS.

5. DON'T TRY TO TAKE ANYTHING AWAY FROM HIM *(don't let him get it in the first place)*.

6. DON'T REACH FOR HIM SUDDENLY.

7. DON'T PUSH HIM OFF YOUR LAP, YOUR PILLOW, A PIECE OF FURNITURE *(instead, move him off with the lead, saying, "Off")*.

8. DON'T GROOM HIM WITHOUT HOLDING THE TRAINING COLLAR UP, TIGHT.

9. DON'T LET HIM ROAM AROUND OUT OF CONTROL WHEN STRANGERS ENTER.

10. DON'T LET HIM ROAM AROUND OUT OF CONTROL WHEN PEOPLE LEAVE IF HIS PATTERN IS TO ATTACK PEOPLE AS THEY GO OUT.

In reading this list, you will undoubtedly recognize those points that correspond to your list of situations in which your dog has threatened or harmed someone. Write those situations on every mirror in the house so that everyone is reminded of them constantly. In the case of the severely aggressive dog, these reminders may save someone from serious injury.

Now work, work, work on the obedience training. Hurry to the level of obedience that permits you to command your dog from thirty feet away and get instant response to your first command. Be demanding and precise. Put in several training sessions a day. Be very encouraging with your dog. Praise him constantly. You must make this program work. Your dog cannot possibly help himself. There is no chance that he will become anything other than worse unless you reverse the pattern and do so quickly.

Aggression Toward Dogs If you are dealing with a problem of aggression toward other dogs, start by having your dog neutered. Then work on the obedience training fast and hard. The first ten days after neutering are extremely significant. Hormones are working out of your dog's system, and he is changing naturally. Make the most of this period; train your dog several times a day, being very precise and demanding.

You will begin to find that you can heel him right past another dog so long as you have him under control *before* encountering the other dog. As long as you continue the control, your dog will remain under control and other dogs will no longer present a temptation—except as playmates, of course.

Keep your dog close to you and under good supervision at all times. When his training is at a very high level and you can expect instant and total obedience on the first command, you're ready to integrate him with other dogs.

Do so by having the other dogs in a fenced area or room before yours arrives. Your dog must enter that room *without* you and unfettered. Have someone else push him through the door, shut it, and stay out. Your dog will no longer attract aggression because he doesn't smell male, and he will find this out very quickly. Then he has a chance to find out that he is no longer aggressive and can have the pleasure of relating to other dogs as he did as a puppy. After a while, you may let the dogs out of the area together or go in and get them. You will find that your dog quickly becomes accustomed to being able to play with other dogs once again.

But a word of warning—about you, the owner. You will be expecting aggression and will communicate your fear to your dog if you are not careful. Train yourself to be prepared without tensing up and thereby setting off *protective* aggression in your dog.

Aggression Among Animals Living Together It's not uncommon to encounter tiffs and outright fights among animals in one household. There are many causes, all of the quite manageable if understood. The most common is "pack activity." Remember, dogs are pack animals; in the pack in nature, things tend to "shake down" of their own accord. But in your home, you influence things and often upset the natural balance. Sometimes it's just plain jealousy, sometimes actual aggression. But in all cases, part of the blame must be placed on your lack of control, your not functioning as pack leader. Fortunately, the situation can be turned around in a hurry.

Start by having *all* dogs in the house neutered to minimize both aggression and pack activity. Keep leads on them at all times when you are home (they won't fight when you're out) so that you may use the leads for control. And train, train, train. Then remember to use training commands to control things when there is the slightest threat of a fight. Once your dogs learn that you can control them and you are no longer upset by their fracases, the fights will stop.

There are also several somewhat unusual forms of aggression worth mentioning:

(a) *Hostility Transference*. The normal aggressive dog, the *true* aggressive dog, is dangerous to anyone and probably has bitten his loved ones even more often than strangers. He will bite when he feels threatend. The situations have been explained previously. But there is also the dog often diagnosed as aggressive who has never bitten his owner, never snapped or growled at him. He is frequently so docile with his owner that you feel his owner could tear him apart limb by limb and never see so much as a curled lip. Yet this dog often attacks others—usually gentle, well-meaning folk—seemingly out of the blue. There may be a pattern—men only, for instance—or there may be none. The only thing for sure is that the dog *never* shows any form of aggression toward his owner, no matter what!

This dog is actually manifesting a transference of hostility. He is *not* aggressive in the normal sense of the word. He simply shows the hostility of his owner on certain occasions, and it would therefore be more appropriate to call his *owner* aggressive. Unfortunately, most owners of dogs in this category are themselves the kind of people who do not display aggression and frequently find it hard to believe that their dogs could be reflecting their (the owner's) own hostility.

If yours is one of these cases, do start training your dog as described for normal aggression problems. But get to work on yourself also. You deserve it, and so does your dog. To say nothing of the rest of the world!

(b) *Anxiety*. As much as insecurity, lack of structure, overactive hormones, and owner hostility are responsible for much aggressive canine behavior, we must also consider the role of human anxiety. I'm not talking about everyday anxieties of a minor, normal nature, but deep-seated anxieties from which some individuals suffer. We occasionally see dogs of a totally pacific nature who exhibit a high degree of nervousness and aggression under certain circumstances. Upon closer inspection, these circumstances usually turn out to be those in which the owner becomes extraordinarily anxious: job situations in which the owner is highly insecure; emotional situations in which the owner becomes absolutely overwrought; physical situations in which the owner becomes terrified. In training dogs as a profession, my colleagues and I see dogs who in the hands of their owners freak out completely on elevators; yet in the hands of someone else, they are calm and otherwise normal. We see dogs who play with visitors, but when the topic of conversation turns, suddenly jump into their owner's lap, snarling at the visitor. These are typical of problems brought on by the dog's sensitivity to his owner's anxieties. When aggression is observed in bitches, this is almost always the reason.

I hope that if you notice your dog exhibiting these symptoms, you will treat them as aggression. But more importantly, for your own peace of mind as well as your dog's, do seek guidance for yourself in dealing with your anxieties.

(c) *Neurological Disorders*. An even more unusual but easily diagnosed form of aggression is that of the dog who is actually experiencing something like seizure activity during his snarling, biting scenes. A normal aggressive dog snarls or bites and backs away, often runs away, but at least desists unless threatened. The dog suffering from the type of neurological disorder I'm describing will often seem to become rigid, growling, blindly biting, remaining rigid and growling for some time, often a frighteningly long time.

This situation is unquestionably scary, but it is quite manageable by the owner who is willing to apply a little more than normal effort and attention to the problem. It is of the utmost importance that the dog be neutered immediately in order to slow down his nervous system a bit and cut out plain old animal aggression. Then you might ask your veterinarian to try an anti-seizure drug. Unfortunately, dogs, like people, react well to one brand, poorly to another. So you may have to try several.

Understand, though, that they are to be anti-convulsive medications, not tranquilizers. Most dogs of this type seem to have an inverse reaction to tranquilizers and become quite dangerous. So try different brands of anti-seizure drugs until you arrive at a suitable brand and dosage.

Training should be done as already described for any other aggressive dog, but with even more care to anticipate problems and with the understanding that results will come slowly. The dog with neurological disorders needs time and a stable atmosphere as well as training and medication. Interestingly enough, however, you will find these dogs are often the most sensitive and rewarding pets once you get the aggression under control. By the way, anti-seizure drugs for dogs are the same as for humans. You can buy them by prescription at your neighborhood drug store very inexpensively.

(d) *The Singular Victim*. Occasionally, a dog shows aggression toward only one specific person. If that person is a normal adult, have him work with the dog on obedience training, following all of the other advice herein. If the person is an older or handicappd adult, you will have to help by doing a lot of work yourself and then dominating the dog strongly in the presence of the victim, followed by your assisting the victim in dominating the dog. Be patient! The human needs your forebearance and encouragement even more than the dog does.

If the victim is a child, the cause will usually be either jealousy, or the child's mistreatment of the dog.

Jealousy in the dog arises when the child, whom the dog considers his contemporary, oftimes a friend, but still an interloper, receives more attention, love, understanding, care, or playthings than the dog. No, I don't expect or recommend that you ignore the child. But fair's fair! Give the dog a few minutes of obedience work every now and then throughout the day. It's easy to diaper a baby while a dog sits and stays—and is complimented for doing it well! It's easy to play with a child on the floor while a dog downs and stays and again is complimented. It's easy to air a child in his carriage with the dog heeling at your side. Don't try to keep the dog's toys and the child's separate. (They aren't going to get any germs from each other's playthings.) It's wasted effort, and the more you do so, the more the child will want the dog's toys and vice versa.

As for "mistreatment," this term covers everything from a child's accidentally poking a finger in the dog's eye to deliberately pulling his hair or tail or whiskers. Some dogs tolerate a lot, as do some people. But most dogs have more than one Achilles heel, and it's unreasonable to expect otherwise.

Teach your child as soon as he begins crawling that the dog is *not* his toy but his friend, to be treated as he himself would like to be treated. Children understand this advice better than you think. Stress it particularly if you have a child at the "terrible two" stage. It's murder on dogs! Especially the male dog that's about nine months of age himself—just beginning to experience "maleness" and the aggression that accompanies it.

I certainly would recommend that any dog that is to live with young children be neutered at six months of age, before aggression rears its ugly head. And most importantly, as your charming baby grows up, get that kid off the dog's back!

A final caution: If your dog has been into any kind of aggressive behavior for many years, you may expect to control the problem, but also do expect to have to keep it under control *yourself* for the rest of his life. There are no miracles in dog training. That is, if you have a dog who has been attacking for some years, you may correct the problem by the means outlined, but at the same time you will have to increase your own level of awareness tremendously so that the situation in which the dog would previously have shown aggression cannot occur in the future without your *first* having the dog completely under control.

This, by the way, is another reason for you to make the list of circumstances in which the dog has demonstrated aggression. This list will help you pinpoint the areas in which *you* must improve your level of awareness and control. The aggressive dog must be *heavily dominated* verbally, and by use of collar and lead when necessary. But he must never be threatened or abused physically. Physical abuse will increase his aggressive behavior once again.

But be assured once again that there are no impossible dogs—only a few owners who will not rise to the level of self-discipline required.

DOGS AND LOVERS

Every once in a while there appears to be a conflict between the dog and the owner's new love interest. Usually these conflicts can be resolved quite easily. The antagonism usually is on the part of a male dog owned by a woman. The dog may growl at a new date, may bite him, or as has happened more than a few times, may lift his leg on the interloper. I'm told that a man is pretty shaken when, as he sits on the sofa sipping a Scotch and trying to be debonair, he suddenly feels something warm and wet trickling down his ankle and into his shoe and sees the dog walking way, tail held high in that "screw you" position.

Worse yet, one client tells of getting out of bed in the morning and tiptoeing off to the kitchen to fix breakfast while her new beau slept. After putting on the coffee, she returned to the bedroom just in time to see her Yorkie lifting his leg, urinating all over the sleeping figure.

Before confronting your dog about his attitude toward your new friend, decide whether or not this guy is really worth it. If he is, he will help, not hinder. He will understand, even commiserate with the dog.

So start on obedience training together. Let your date feed the dog whenever he visits. Let him walk the dog and generally do the things the dog likes most. Just be sure the dog doesn't become so attached to him that he switches homes!

Another word of caution: if things escalate from bad to worse (which can happen only if your new friend does not work with the dog in good faith), don't immediately think of giving up the dog. He's your genuine friend. His judgment is really quite good. Look at the situation and the tensions caused by the more recent addition, bearing in mind that relationships which depend upon *either* party's disposing of a pet are unhealthy to begin with and can only lead to further tyranny. How many clients tell us of pets they "got rid of" as part of a marriage contract, only to realize years later that the one to go should have been the human! After all, if a prospective husband isn't understanding about your dog, what can his attitude possibly be toward your own mother?

12
Problems You Didn't Expect

THE DRUG SCENE

Unfortunately, our dogs must live in the same drug-oriented society we do. And suffer accordingly.

Since people live on tranquilizers, drop acid, take ups and downs, O.D., sniff coke, and smoke pot or hash, they assume it's all right for dogs too. Admittedly, some people just happen to leave the stuff out and the dogs, naturally, get into it. In other cases, though, people knowingly give such a substance to their dogs or smoke it in their presence. The result? The dogs are high on Saturday night (like their owners) and down on Sunday morning.

Your dog can't cope with this routine and shouldn't have to. He can't understand his highs and lows, can't control his bladder when in either state, has no concept of what a "bummer" is except that it's pretty terrifying. So leave him out of—along with the kids.

THE SPY IN THE BEDROOM

The Dog's Place in Your Love Life

Thank God dogs can't talk. But the way some people carry on, you'd think they could.

Clients are forever telling us of shutting the dog out of the bedroom during lovemaking and then wondering why he deposits a pile of you-know-what right at the door where someone will step in it in his bare feet on the way to the bathroom.

If you're one of the many who have had this experience and spent the end of what started out to be a great romantic evening scraping dog shit out from under your toe nails, ah, come on, let him watch. Who's he going to tell, anyway?

One client, when confronted with the necessity of tying the dog to the bed for housebreaking purposes, rearranged the bedroom furniture to place a dresser between the dog and the bed so that the dog couldn't watch. Then the dog's veterinarian suggested I teach the dog not only how to untie himself but also to use a Polaroid camera. After all, those people have got to be doing something interesting!

Seriously, just tie the dog to the foot of the bed, either so he can sit on the end of the bed and watch or—if you still have a few hangups—on the floor where he *can't* watch. But if he's on the floor, at least give him a chewie or leave the TV on for him to watch.

One thing I don't recommend, however, is permitting or—worse yet—teaching your dog to participate. That's sick. And it can be embarassing (as it was to one dog owner I know) when your in-laws come to visit and the dog climbs in bed with them and. . . .

NEW BABY IN THE HOUSE

A new baby in the house should be just as much a pleasure to the dog as to the adults. Remember, when the baby first comes home from the hospital, he will be no more to the dog than a smell that cries; he won't be moving around yet, won't be interfering yet.

So before the baby even arrives in the house, accustom the dog to the new family member by bringing home one of the baby's *dirty* diapers (this is a fairly accepted practice, so the nurse won't think you're crazy when you ask her to put one in a doggy bag) and leaving it around on the floor with the dog for a few days.

Then all the dog has to do is worry about the crying, which he will come to ignore fast enough. His only other problem will be to adjust to all the attention given that little creature who smells and cries. Simply make sure that all the people who come to see the baby greet the dog first. He will be delighted and think this party is being given for him!

Above all, don't neglect your dog's obedience work at this crucial time. It's a good thing for the new father to be working on obedience training during those few lonely days while mother and child are still at the hospital. When the child arrives at home, continue this attention to the dog, so that he doesn't feel left out. And nothing more will be required.

STOP CHEWING YOUR NAILS!

Dogs that Chew Their Coats,
Lick Their Feet and Skin, Gnaw at Their
Nails, Scratch, and Have Seizures

What ever made you think dogs are less neurotic than people? Less sensitive to pressure? Forget it!

Dogs chew their coats and flesh down to the bone. Or lick their feet and pull at the hair between the pads. Or gnaw at their nails and even pull them out. Or scratch away endlessly.

Yet the veterinarian finds nothing wrong, calls it "nonspecific dermatitis"; gives a shot that relieves the condition (but makes the dog drink a good deal of water and urinate accordingly). The condition must indeed be treated physically. But it must also be treated psychologically.

The dog is showing signs of tension picked up from the environment in which he lives. Obviously, getting your act together will help. Chances are, however, that you won't do so overnight. But you can do obedience work overnight. Two twenty-minute, effective obedience sessions daily will bring the situation under control, save the dog further discomfort, and save you some money on veterinary bills. To say nothing of saving the veterinarian from having to do all those fruitless skin scrapings.

Similarly, the seizure-prone dog is subject to the stress around him. Seizure activity (such as epilepsy) can frequently be reduced in severity and frequency by neutering, medication, and obedience training. Equally important, though, is the lessening of stress in the *owner's* life, thereby relaxing the dog's environment.

Our organization has for many years boarded in our homes a good number of dogs and cats who in their own homes chew themselves, scratch constantly, suffer asthma attacks, gnaw at their nails, lick away endlessly, and have seizures. Never has one shown any of these symptoms when with us.

Draw your own conclusions. And do something about it.

PUT HIS NAME ON THE DOOR

Moving to a New Home

How frequently I hear of the "perfect" dog who fell apart upon moving to a new home! Many dogs, like many people, find moving a rather unnerving experience. Dogs who have never barked before now yap at every noise. Dogs who calmly stayed home alone all day every day suddenly become hysterical when their owners get ready to leave for work—and then howl all day. Dogs who have never chewed a thing suddenly destroy a wall. Dogs who have never had an "accident" since puppyhood suddenly urinate in sixteen different places in the new living room. All these surprises and more may await you if you don't give a little consideration to your dog *before* moving.

Many well-meaning dog owners "spare" the dog the hassle of the move by leaving him elsewhere and then suddenly dropping him into the new environment and immediately walking out themselves. Others arrive, dog on lead, and again dump him among the packing cartons and go off for a hamburger.

Have a heart! He doesn't know what's going on. Ideally, you should take the dog to the new home frequently before you move in, walk him through it, and *do obedience work there*. This obedience suggestion is the most important since it will make your dog feel secure immediately. If you cannot take him to the new home ahead of time, take him along as soon as possible. Walk him around; do obedience work with him in his new environment; put out his dish filled with water, his bed, and his toys; determine his den area and put enough of your things in there to let him know you're staying. Don't walk out immediately and leave him.

Try to have someone with the dog for at least a day before you leave him alone. And don't leave him alone without doing at least half an hour of obedience work with him and then putting him in his den.

You may have a sense of permanence the minute you sign that staggering check for rent or mortgage payment. Your dog doesn't even have a checking account, much less know his new home is indeed home!

WHICH CHAIR IS WHOSE?

Yes, it is possible to let your dog sit in one chair and not another. It's possible to let him sleep on the bed at night but not sleep on the white velvet sofa when you're sitting there reading (no, he won't sleep there when you're out, because he'll be in his den). And it's even possible to let the dog sleep on the bed at night and *not* get the linens dirty.

First of all, decide which pieces of furniture the dog may get on, if any. The rules, once established, must be maintained by *everyone* in the house. It's not fair to expect the dog to sit on the sofa on Monday and not Tuesday. Once you've decided, simply permit him to sit on those you wish and tell him, "Off," when he gets on one you don't want him on. Remove him from it. If he has a penchant for climbing on the forbidden sofa every time you leave the room, simply upend the seat cushions. Few dogs bother to do anything about it.

If you would like your dog to sleep on the bed at night bu

not soil the spread or linens, buy a few fitted sheets and put one on *over* the spread. It will bear the brunt of the dirt, and you can throw it in the wash however often you wish. Just think: if you get a few permanent-press patterned sheets during a sale, you can keep things clean without disturbing the decor of your room or having to iron any more sheets.

And I don't even want to hear about the dogs that sleep *under* the covers!

TRAVELING WITH YOUR DOG

Traveling with your dog is just about like traveling with a young child, except that it gets easier more quickly.

America travels, and travels, and travels—with its dogs as well as its children, mothers-in-law, bicycles, and canoes. Motels have begun to expect dogs, and the majority welcome your dog since is the only way to get *you*. All the major chains accept dogs. But if you're planning to stay at a non-chain-member motel, do check ahead to make sure Superdog is welcome. Some motels accept a dog on the condition that he will not be left in the room unattended, which may limit your vacation activities somewhat.

Pack your dog's food, some water just in case it's not available on the road between stops, his grooming implements, an extra collar and lead, his bowl, an old towel in event of rain, some Kaopectate (better to have it and not need it than need it and not have it!), some chewies, infant suppositories, and newspapers if he's paper-trained. Make sure he has an identification tag on his collar and that his vaccinations are current. If you plan to travel outside your state, get a health certificate from your veterinarian to meet other states' requirements.

Detroit has installed all sorts of safety gadgets for human passengers but none for your dog. So you must compensate. In case of a sudden stop or accident, your dog, for his own safety as well as yours, should not be able to fly around. If you have a large dog or several dogs and a station wagon, get, at an automotive supply store, what is called a "dog barrier," actually a sort of fence that fits with suction cups across the wagon behind the seat so that the dog has his own area in which to ride but cannot fly forward. If you don't have a wagon, develop the habit of putting the dog in the same seat each time. If he is accustomed to lying down and sleeping, fine. Otherwise, use his lead to tie him to the seat belt in his seat so that he can't fly around or breathe down your neck. Also, he'll feel much more secure this way.

Obviously, if the dog is *tied* to a seat belt, he must have his lead on, since the lead will be used for tying. However, be sure you never leave his lead on if he's alone in the car. And be sure to remove the lead if you put the dog behind a dog barrier. But get that lead back on before you open the door to take your dog out of the car! And while you're at it, use that obedience training to teach him to sit and stay in the car until he receives permission to get out.

Then there's the dog who gets car sick. First, before you decide there's something wrong with the dog, examine your own driving. We have noticed that many dogs become ill only when being "chauffeured" by people who repeatedly start and stop suddenly. If you're not at fault, though, you have to start preventing the dog's *being sick* so that he doesn't *"think sick."* Do so by not feeding him or giving him water for at least sixteen hours (twenty-four if necessary) before taking him in the car.

If he gags in the car, ignore it. If he vomits a little saliva (white) or bile (yellow), clean it up and say nothing. Just keep treating him as if everything were normal, and it soon will be. If possible, give him several short drives before embarking on an all-day trip. But in any case, remember that car sickness is a state of mind. Once your dog has had several positive experiences (created by not having food or water in his stomach), he will gradually stop "thinking sick." Then you'll be able to feed him closer to travel time. It's never a good idea, though, to feed and water a dog immediately before setting out.

If you must park and leave the dog in the car at restaurants along the way, try to park within sight of the area where you will be sitting so as to make sure the car isn't broken into and the dog stolen. Dog-napping is very common. The best prevention, of course, is a locked car and an alarm system.

You must, naturally, shut the windows except for an inch or so of ventilation space. But be sure not to leave the dog in such a situation for more than a few minutes during hot weather, and certainly don't park in the sun. Many dogs die of heat prostration every summer because their owners thoughtlessly leave them in closed cars that soon get overheated. Cold, on the other hand, presents very little problem to the dog for the period of time you're likely to leave him while you dine. No, you needn't bring him back a hot buttered rum!

I do not recommend that you travel by air with your dog unless he is small enough to fit in the case the airline permits you to keep at your seat. Check with the airline when making a reservation. Each has its own rules. In any event, shipping a dog in the baggage compartment is extremely dangerous and should be avoided at all costs.

A possible alternative, if you cannot drive, is to take the train or bus. You can take dogs in bedrooms and compartments on trains, and dogs in carrying cases on most buses. A word of advice though: get the carrying case several weeks in advance, and get the dog accustomed to it by putting him in it for short periods each day and carrying him around a bit, rewarding him with praise and a tidbit each time. You should begin to find him crawling into the case whenever you leave it open, demanding that you "get a move on!"

DOG MEETS DOG

A New Dog in the House

As soon as you have *one* perfect dog, you'll begin thinking how much fun he could have with a playmate. You're right!

It really is no more work to have two or three than one—except of course, for the grooming. But before you add to your pet population, be sure your first dog is indeed well-trained. Then look around for another.

When you have one pet, it is easier if your second is not a tiny puppy so that you don't have to go through the paper-training stage while you have an adult, outdoor-trained dog in the house. In fact, a second dog a year old or more will probably suit everyone best.

Be sure your first dog is neutered (spayed or castrated) before introducing the newcomer. Likewise, have the new addition neutered before taking him home if possible. There is much less pack activity and aggression between neutered animals.

Let the dogs get acquainted on neutral territory: a park, building hallway, neighbor's yard, wherever. Once they seem relaxed together, take them into your home, but leave their leads on, dragging behind them. Be prepared for some rough play, running, jumping, and so on, and for housebreaking "accidents" resulting from excitement and exercise. Also be prepared for housebreaking "incidents" to establish territory and dominance. If things seem to get out of hand, just grab the leads and give a couple of hard jerks, yelling, "No!" If necessary, tie the dogs apart until they calm down. Let them sleep tied and start all over again under better control.

Be aware that the chasing and playing will calm down as the pets adjust to one another in a day or two. Just leave those leashes on when you're home, and put any limits on the play that seem necessary.

When you go out, confine the dogs *together*, not separately. Obviously, leave them in an indestructible room to begin with. And, wonder of wonders: the smaller the room, the less the wilderness. So don't think two dogs need twice as much space as one. Hardly!

In all probability you'll see some status maneuvering between the pets. Keep out of it. You cannot change the dominance patterns inherent in their natures. It doesn't really matter who's on top—they'll work it out. You just relax and stop worrying about who has all the toys and who has none. That's life.

But do get to work immediately with obedience training for your new dog, alternating training periods between the two of them. Soon they will sit and stay, down and stay, stand and stay together. Then they'll come together. And finally heel together. And you're home free.

DOG MEETS CAT

Once upon a time every farm had cats in the barn and dogs in the pasture and kitchen. Neither the cats nor the dogs nor the farmer ever thought it strange that all lived in harmony, for all were "God's creatures," and that was that.

But as we became an urban nation, our agrarian past receding quickly, we became "cat people" and "dog people." As if there were a difference!

Now, however, with the vast animal population depositing litters and strays at our doors, we are put in contact with all domestic creatures—who don't stop to ask whether it is the door of a "cat person" or a "dog person." And we find we do indeed love them equally—differently perhaps, but equally.

This situation can at times present some problems, though. If you're about to get a cat and dog together for the first time, you may be experiencing all kinds of trepidations—and wisely so. They are not likely to kill one another, but the tearing around can get out of hand fast.

Usually a cat, confronted with a new dog, will leap from one safe perch to another, observing the dog, perhaps even approaching it curiously. The dog in turn will probably think this is all a great game and go bounding after the cat. And next thing you know, your precious knicknacks are flying, the cat is hissing and howling and scratching, and the dog is wondering why in the world you're so upset.

To avoid such chaos, put a lead at least six feet long on the dog before introducing the cat. Then if necessary, you can control the dog and thus the cat also. The cat will not leap about wildly if the dog does not give chase. You will find that if you keep the lid on for a short time, your animals will form a friendship quickly and adjust their play to what you can live with. The worst that can happen is that they'll ignore each other or do an occasional bit of teasing.

Other situations you must be aware of when cat and dog share a house arise from the need to keep cat litter available as well as cat food.

To avoid chaos when cat and dog meet, put a six-foot lead on the dog before introducing them. If necessary, you can then control the dog and thus the cat also. The cat will not leap about wildly if the dog does not give chase.

Obviously, if the cat food is reachable, the dog will eat it, leaving none for the cat and upsetting the dog's own diet and housebreaking at the same time. It is therefore necessary to feed the cat in a place that it can jump to readily and safely but which is out of reach of the dog. If your dog is small, the kitchen counter will do. Otherwise, how about the top of the refrigerator?

Then there's the litter. If there is a dog in this world who doesn't love to eat cat feces from the litter box, we haven't met him. Most dogs would prefer this "delicacy" to anything you can offer. So put the litter—preferably in one of the closed-type litter boxes—up high enough on a table, platform, shelf, or whatever, that the dog can't reach it. You will find that if you put a turkish towel under the box, the cat will wipe his feet and not track litter around the house. Also, many cats are just as happy to use a swirl of toilet paper, which can then be flushed down the john. And some even prefer newspaper. If yours is accustomed to litter and you would like to change to newspaper or toilet paper, put the paper in the box with litter on top of it and gradually cut down the amount of litter to zero. Happy owner, happy cat, neat house!

THE DEATH OF A LOVED ONE

The loss of a loved one—whether human, cat, or dog—can be extremely traumatic for your dog.

He may react in any of several ways. He may simply withdraw and grieve in solitude. He may become very restless, wandering about the house whining, then barking and howling when you leave. He may suddenly have housebreaking or destructiveness problems.

You can do many things to help.

If your dog lost his canine or feline friend, you may get him another companion—not a replacement (you cannot "replace" anything or anyone), simply a new one.

If he lost his human, you can only try to compensate. Take him places; give him lots of attention.

In all cases, it's most important to give him a lot of precise, demanding obedience work as a distraction. Praise him for his performance. Above all, don't ever go out and leave him alone without first having spent some time working with him to dispel his depression before he must be alone.

Obviously, specific problems like housebreaking or destructiveness or barking when the dog is alone also require the solutions indicated in the appropriate chapters of this book.

Follow the suggestions, and remember that time—with a little help from you—does indeed heal all.

13
Care

HOT-WEATHER CARE

Cats can generally tolerate higher temperatures than humans with no noticeable effects other than lethargy.

Dogs can also tolerate hot weather but do require a little assistance from the human element.

First, *don't* make the mistake of shaving off the dog's coat for the summer in the hope of keeping him cool. Your dog's coat naturally contains dead air spaces that insulate him against both heat and cold. In addition, the coat protects his skin from sunburn and from the bites of insects including mosquitoes, which can carry heart worm. If you must keep the coat short in order to be able to manage the grooming, by all means do so. But don't shave the dog down to his skin.

Instead of simply filling your dog's water dish with water from the tap, fill it with a tray of ice cubes and add a cup or so of cold water, letting the melting ice keep the water cold for sometime; then add more ice cubes.

In addition, keep a plant-misting spray bottle full of water in the refrigerator. Periodically throughout the day, spray the dog with this cold water, lifting the coat and spraying the water to the skin as much as possible. If the dog has a long coat, brush the coat up against the grain as you spray so that the water reaches down to the roots. Obviously, you will also prevent matting of the coat if you brush as you spray. In fact, you will find this a very healthy practice to stimulate the dog's coat and skin.

When you go out, it's not necessary to leave the air conditioner on for the dog and run up enormous electric bills. Instead, spray the dog thoroughly with the cold water and leave him in a bathroom where he can lie on the cold tile floor. Also, give him a dish of ice cubes, no water added this time. They will melt and provide cold drinking water for hours to come, and he can chew them if he wishes. In either case, he will keep cool while lying, well sprayed, on the cold tile floor, partaking of his ice cubes, comfortable for many hours in the warmest weather, without your supporting the local electric company.

In case you haven't guessed it, I recommend that you leave the dog at home rather than take him with you where you'll have to leave him in a parked car in hot weather. Even a few minutes in the shade with the windows partially rolled up on a warm day can be too much and cause heat prostration.

If during hot weather you must take your dog with you (on vacation, for instance) at least spray him well before leaving him, park in the shade, leave the windows open a few inches, and get back to the car *quickly*. If possible, as suggested previously, give the dog a dish of ice cubes to make the heat a little more bearable.

BASIC GROOMING

The grooming of your dog indicates the pride you have in him, just as your own personal grooming indicates the pride you have in yourself. So if you're sitting there in your underwear, beer can in hand, grimy Poodle in your lap, well, at least sit up a little straighter as you read on.

If you cannot groom your dog yourself (and you can at least brush him, no matter how intricate the rest of his coiffure may be), have him groomed as often as necessary to keep him handsome, clean, and lovable even to strangers. He'll feel better that way, take more pleasure in his relationship with you, and become more attached to you, knowing you're proud of him.

Each breed is groomed in its own way. The best way to

learn what's necessary for your breed is to ask the breeder (not pet shop) from whom you got him. If you did not get your dog from a breeder, then the best way is to watch the handlers at a dog show or read a *good* book on the grooming of *your* breed.

There is at least one dog show in every part of the U. S. almost every weekend. To get a schedule of shows, write to the American Kennel Club, 51 Madison Avenue, New York, New York 10010, asking for a show calendar. (This same calendar will indicate obedience trials as well.) It's free.

To get the name of a *good* book on grooming your breed, write to the American Kennel Club and ask for the name and address of the secretary of the club for your breed. There is a club for every breed: for instance, Chihuahua Club of America, American Shetland Sheepdog Association, Shih Tzu Club of America, and so on. Then simply write to the secretary, requesting the name of the book. You will find that these books differ greatly from the cheap booklets sold in pet shops, which often offer incorrect advice.

No matter what your breed, however, I can give you some general dog-grooming advice you may find helpful.

First, buy a good quality dog shampoo. They come in colors such as apricot, silver, and white for dogs of those colors. There is a special formula for wire-coated dogs like some of the Terriers. And there are good tearless, protein shampoos for dogs not needing any of those just mentioned. In any case, a tearless shampoo should be used around the dog's eyes.

Your dog's coat must be *completely tangle-free* before bathing. Any minor tangles left in at bath time will be major mats by the end of the bath.

During the dog's bath, do leave his training collar on so that you have some way to control him. You may also find it helpful to put cotton in his ears so they don't fill with water. If he keeps shaking the cotton out, then just be sure you dry the ears with swabs or cotton after his bath.

Put a rubber bath mat in the bottom of the tub, so the dog won't slip and become frightened. Use a hand shower (don't fill the tub), preferably the European "telephone shower" type, since the rubber ones always seem to slip off the faucet, spurting water all over the master, rather than the dog.

Start by spraying water down through the coat, wetting it thoroughly. Work well-diluted shampoo *down through the coat; don't rub the coat in various directions or mats will develop during the bathing process* if your dog has a long coat. Rinse by spraying water *down through the coat*. If necessary, shampoo and rinse again. In order to be sure all shampoo is removed from the coat and to leave the coat softer and more glistening, pour over the dog a solution of 10% white vinegar or lemon juice and 90% water. Rinse out this solution along with the soap it will remove. Then squeeze excess water out of the coat with your hands.

Thereafter, if the coat is short, you may rub it dry. If, however, your dog has a long coat (such as a Poodle, Lhasa, Yorkie, Old English, or Afghan) pour on a coat-conditioning creme rinse, well-diluted. Rinse again or not, depending upon the instructions on the rinse. Then *blot* the coat with a towel; *do not rub*, or mats may form. Long coats must be dried with a blower type of hair drier, combing or brushing each section thoroughly as it dries. *Do not dry any section without combing or brushing as it dries*. This procedure will leave an airy, flowing coat that will be easy to keep mat-free for weeks to come.

It is recommended that heavily coated dogs be brushed and combed daily. The entire shampoo-rinse process should be repeated on long-coated dogs when the comb will no longer pass through the coat effortlessly.

While you're at it, don't forget to cut nails and clean ears. Most often, when people say a dog "smells," they're really talking about the odor of dirty ears. In drop-eared dogs particularly, matter builds up inside the ear quickly and must be removed with alcohol (or oil) on cotton. Certain breeds—like Poodles, Shih Tuz, Lhasas, Wheatens, Yorkies, and Old English—must have hair removed from the ear canal periodically. Ask your veterinarian to show you how this is done so that you may avoid ear infections and odor.

THE NON-ALLERGENIC PET

Most people who are allergic to dogs or cats are actually allergic to the dander (flakes of dead skin we generally call dandruff) these animals leave behind. So you must be prepared to treat two areas in order to allergy-proof your pet: 1) the pet himself, and 2) his environment (your home).

Expect to vacuum the house several times before you pick up all the accumulation of dander and dead hair carrying dander. If your dog has been sleeping on the beds, wash the spreads, sheets, blankets, and so on. If he has been sleeping on furniture, vacuum it thoroughly several times. With each vacuuming, over succesive days, you will substantially decrease the amount of dander that is floating around.

Now for the pet himself. First of all, buy in a pet shop a coat conditioner of the type that is added to his food. No, you shouldn't just add some sort of cooking oil or bacon fat. Those substances are not properly balanced to suit a dog's needs. Just buy the coat conditioner and put it in your dog's food every day. It's an absolute necessity to use it to decrease and finally eliminate excessive dander.

Then shampoo your dog, following the bathing directions given earlier in this chapter through the shampoo step and the vinegar or lemon rinse. Next blot the coat with a towel, leaving the pet in the tub. Thereafter pour over him a solution of one part fabric softener (the type that is added to the *rinse* water, not to the original wash itself) to six parts water. *Do not rinse this off*. Let it soak in, and then towel dry the pet and use a hair dryer if necessary. The fabric softener rinse will keep down the dander for as long as four weeks, perhaps more. I suggest that you bathe your dog again, using the fabric softener rinse, about four weeks after the first such treatment. Thereafter, do it as often as seems necessary— that is, whenever you begin to experience an allergic reaction again. For some people, that's every three weeks, for others six to eight weeks, probably depending upon the type of coat and skin condition of the dog.

The identical treatment, including coat conditioner in food, may be used on a cat.

Remember, it will take at least ten days to pick up all the dander that is around the house, if you vacuum several times during that period, so don't expect the reaction to stop the minute you treat the pet. You must also keep treating the house.

14
How to Acquire a Dog

There are several good ways to acquire a dog (or cat) once you have decided that you really desire one. But before you set out to select your pet, give some thought to the following:

1. What size dog are you capable of caring for? How much exercise can you provide? How large is your home?

2. How much grooming are you willing to do? Can you spare an hour a day to care for a long-coated breed, or would you prefer a short-haired breed requiring little grooming? Can you afford professional grooming? Check the rates in your town or city before deciding?

3. How much can you afford to spend on food? Obviously, large dogs eat more. And what about veterinary bills? Find out what they are likely to run in your community.

4. Have you the money to pay for neutering? If not, plan to acquire a dog or cat already neutered or at least eligible for low-cost neutering through a nearby neutering clinic or humane society.

5. Do you have time to housebreak a tiny puppy? Also, have you the patience for a wee one?

6. How do your children behave with pets? Try to pick

a dog sturdy enough to take the wear and tear of living with children.

Now, *where* to acquire the pet:

1. Humane societies: these organizations have available every age, size, breed, or mixed breed of dog or cat at reasonably low cost to you. Many have neutered animals or will help you neuter them inexpensively. This is generally the best place to acquire an adult dog or cat, as they will have several available and often know a good deal about their personalities and backgrounds. Remember, an adult dog or cat will be quickly housebroken and will be beyond the teething-chewing stage. Its personality and looks will be established. You never know what a puppy will grow up to be!

2. Adoption ads in your local newspaper: these ads are placed either by current owners seeking new homes for unwanted pets or by humane workers who have taken responsibility for someone else's pet. Remember, the fact that someone is giving up a pet doesn't make the *pet* undesirable; it simply tells you the people in question should not have the pet.

3. Professional breeders: reputable professional breeders own good-quality, healthy, pedigreed breeding stock. They show their animals and become knowledgeable about the breed and their own breed lines as well. They do *not* breed pet quality deliberately. Animals of pet quality result from the honest attempt to breed show quality animals, occasionally producing some pet quality as well. Obviously, you can also buy show quality animals from these breeders if you're interested in showing a dog and have the time and money to do so.

Breeders generally advertise in local papers. You may also get a list of breeders of a given breed by writing to the

American Kennel Club, 51 Madison Avenue, New York, N. Y. 10010.

In answering ads in local papers, be very careful not to patronize those people who have simply bred two pets—what we call "back-yard breeders." These matings seldom produce a pet of reliable quality and certainly should be discouraged.

Pet shops are the worst places to buy a dog or cat. Reputable breeders do not "wholesale" their animals to pet shops, and you therefore cannot buy a quality pet in a pet shop. Rather, you are buying a very poor quality, *expensive* pet bred on a scale similar to that on which General Motors produces cars—mass production. Animals, unlike cars, are living creatures and cannot be mass-produced successfully, since mass production of necessity precludes breeding for stable disposition, good health, and type (what a breed *should* look like). The few animals arriving at pet shops from someone's kitchen are the "back-yard breeder's" mistakes. You don't want them either from the back yard or the pet shop.

However you acquire a pet, try to select an alert animal from clean, well-maintained surroundings. The liveliest in the litter will generally remain that way all his life and is most likely to be a problem as well as a pleasure—so beware! Make sure the pet has been given inoculations appropriate to its age—and take it to a veterinarian as soon as you have acquired it. The person from whom you receive the pet should certainly agree to your returning it if your veterinarian so recommends because of health problems.

A new pet should be one of the greatest pleasures in your life, if you have considered and chosen well.

15
Society's Reflection

This domestic animal, who is a gift to man to provide him his own reflection, is he not telling us that our society and the individuals who comprise it are in deep trouble?

Millions of homeless cats and dogs roam the country, only to meet death from starvation or under car wheels, or with luck, in the decompression chambers of humane societies (some 25 million are "gotten rid of" annually at a cost of $100 million). En route to their horrible end, these animals breed more of their kind, kill other animals, and frighten children and adults alike. Yet *they* know no contentment until the day their dead eyes stare up to meet ours as we drive by another lifeless form on the highway.

And even those who do have homes, food, and warmth frequently are scarcely any better off because of the human world in which they must live, but in which *their* needs are not met and contentment is even less likely than for the stray.

Action for change is certainly in order. In recent years we have begun to hear a great deal more about our pet animals (not ourselves, of course) becoming a problem. *All* of us who own dogs are criticized for the mess on the sidewalks in big cities, although everyone who thinks about it surely recognizes the mess is the result of only a few thoughtless dog owners. On the other hand, no one is commonly blamed for the vast pet overpopulation, for which many, many pet owners are indeed responsible. Both situations are going to destroy us (remember Iceland, in which no dogs are permitted?) if we don't turn them around quickly. Now that you have solved your own pet's problems and become so knowledgeable about animal behavior, why *not* move on to helping society as a whole?

Since strays obviously suffer terribly and contribute to the overpopulation problem and the litter situation, let's start with strays and overpopulation in general.

Everyone asks, "Where do strays come from?"

Early in December, a child's mother and father discussed a perfect Christmas gift for him: a puppy. They didn't know anything about dogs and really weren't terribly interested. The puppy would be a Christmas present to teach the child "responsibility," feeding his pet, walking him, grooming him. So they went to a neighborhood pet shop full of puppies, where they picked out a cute little thing that set them back plenty, but where no questions were asked about their reasons for buying a dog, their experience with dogs, their knowledge of feeding, training, grooming, or even whether their lease permitted a pet. After all, when people want to buy a commodity, well, just take the money and put it in the cash register.

The child of course was delighted to find this cuddly bundle under the tree, ribbon 'round his neck. It was indeed a wonderful Christmas.

By New Year's Day, however, the novelty had begun to wear off. No one knew anything about housebreaking. In fact, they all had always supposed dogs just somehow got housebroken if you took them outside occasionally. (*We* all know better!) And as you might guess, the child was too young to take the pup out at night, and not really interested in the "responsibility" part of it.

By the end of the first week of January, the father was asking around at the office to see whether someone would like to have the pup. Those who had no experience with dogs sensed that they couldn't take over in this situation. Those with experience already had dogs or didn't want to housebreak a puppy in cold weather. The father began to get desperate. Finally, one night he returned home to a great tirade from his wife about her cleaning up after the pup all day. The dog had to go! So the father took the pup off to a park, where he left him, telling himself some kindly "dog lover" would eventually find him and take him in.

The dog became a stray, wandering the parks and streets, living on garbage as best he could, and finally breeding frequently.

In June a prosperous city family moved to the beach for the summer, and the mother thought how nice it would be for the children to have a pet for the summer. She went to the local humane society and adopted a funny little puppy, who did bring the children many pleasant hours, running on the beach, playing at the edge of the surf. Housebreaking certainly was no problem on the beach.

Come Labor Day, the family returned to the city. With the summer over and school about to begin, the pup was no longer needed to entertain the children. She was left behind on the beach. She became a stray, but with all the summer people gone, there was no garbage to eat.

A young man, bearded and long-haired, was walking his Shepherd across town to the park. The dog stayed near his side along the way to the park, even though he was not on a leash. But once in the park, he picked up the scent of a bitch in season and ran off, heedless of his master's cries, interested only in that compelling smell.

Eventually, he too became a stray, joining a dog pack living in the park, foraging for food, often not finding any and becoming quite hostile from his increasing hunger.

The farmer had always loved his Collie/Shepherd and was pleased when she seemed to be pregnant. He looked forward to a litter of pups around the farm. And sure enough there soon were nine. They were cute, fun to watch, trailing around after their dam. They grew up, of course, but still were pleasant companions. The farmer never thought to put a leash on them or keep them fenced in. With the passing of several months, they began to roam, eventually forgetting home completely.

Soon they joined a pack of feral (wild) dogs, moving from farm to farm, killing sheep and chickens for food, and of course, breeding at will. These are the rural strays. . . .

All of these will, in addition, reproduce themselves many times over, thus increasing the stray population even further.

Stories like these will probably give you several immediate ideas to help prevent an increase in the stray population:

1. Encourage friends to buy puppies only after much thought and then from knowledgeable breeders or responsible shelters that can give them the assistance they will need with a new pup.

2. Assist those needing help in training new pets.

3. Discourage all but the most experienced, professional breeders from adding to the population. Let your friends know you won't take puppies off their hands. Suggest that before using their pets to show the children "the miracle of birth," they show them the horrors of death in the local humane society's decompression chambers.

4. Neuter your own pets, and encourage your friends to do likewise. Pressure local government and humane organizations for the establishment of low-cost neutering programs if there are none in your community.

5. Let your friends know that even if they buy a pet-shop animal just to get it out of the pet shop, as many humane individuals do, that animal will shortly be replaced with two more. It is in the long run less cruel to animals in general to be more cruel and leave that particular pup or kitten in the shop, forcing the owner to take a loss.

6. Join an obedience-training club in your area so that you may learn that much more about animal behavior and thereby be of even greater help to your friends and neighbors.

7. And most importantly, visit your local humane organizations, find out what you as a volunteer can do to help them. Money is always needed. But

before contributing, spend some time there, find out what happens. Do they have an active adoption service? Do they neuter *all* animals before they are adopted, or if the animals are too young for neutering, at least require the adoptive owners to return them for neutering by six months of age—and follow up to be sure it is done? It is foolish to contribute time or money to an organization that perpetuates itself by giving out unneutered animals.

While discussing these points with friends, family, neighbors, humane workers, and veterinarians, you will find yourself in an ideal position to cover the subject of dog litter as well and to assist your neighborhood and city in better coping with what everyone refers to as "the mess."

As you have already learned from reading about dog foods and their effect on housebreaking, dog owners should be encouraged to feed their dogs a diet based on kibble and to avoid soft-moist foods at all costs, thereby decreasing the *quantity* of fecal matter to be dealt with. Then all you have to do is get the litter into the right place!

1. Many cities have clean-up laws. Many dog owners clean up, law or no. An easy way to do so is: with a small plastic bag over your hand pick up the feces, pull the bag over the feces (turning the bag inside out over your hand), and then close the bag with a tie and dispose of it properly.

2. If your area has alternate-side-of-the-street parking and street cleaning, encourage dog owners to walk their dogs on the side to be cleaned next. Lest they forget which that is, handouts may be printed cheaply, simply listing the desirable side on given days and times. Make sure one is slipped under the door of every resident so *all* know what effort is being made—don't distribute only to the dog owners!

3. Many neighborhood associations have found it

practicable to pick a sizable gutter area—such as that in front of a fire hydrant where parking is prohibited anyway—paint a wide stripe around it (with the permission of the local police or traffic department, of course) with the word "Dogs" within and let all dog owners in the vicinity know "this is the place!" Then one building superintendent or resident is paid (or volunteers) to clean up the feces twice a day with a scoop made for that purpose.

4. In areas where there are heavily traveled streets, it is frequently advisable to walk dogs on those streets during a hiatus in traffic and let the feces be ground under the wheels.

5. Some areas with sufficient water pressure will allow residents to open hydrants daily and wash down entire stretches of street, clearing not only dog litter but dirt and dust as well. Certainly, this may be done weekly or monthly to prevent accumulations.

Along with implementing the foregoing points, you will have to create an information program for dog owners so that they learn *how* to teach their pets to defecate in the agreed-upon areas, to do so quickly, to wait until reaching these areas, not using trees, lawns, parks, plants, sidewalks, crosswalks, bus stops, building entrance areas, and so on. The illustration is of literature used in such a program in New York City. It may obviously be adapted to the needs of any given locale.

If necessary, city-block associations should be prepared to put guards around trees and plants to prevent dogs from urinating and defecating on them during the educational period—education of the *dog owners*, that is. At the same time, you often must make it clear to the owners that *their* permitting their dogs to use inappropriate areas as a toilet is contrary to law and that, if necessary, the law will be enforced. Here again, it is most important that the pressure be brought to bear by the *dog-owning public* so as to avoid out-and-out antagonism. All dog owners certainly would like to see their dogs urinate and defecate in acceptable places, but few know how to accomplish the goal or even how to select a suitable area and get the cooperation of their neighbors.

Armed with the knowledge you have gained, you may indeed change the reflection your community's animals provide of its human inhabitants.

TO KEEP
OUR PARKS
& SIDEWALKS
C L E A N !

**DOG TRAINING
BY WIDMER**
314 West 78th Street
New York, New York
(212) 874-1261

HOW TO STREET TRAIN YOUR DOG
(Teach him to defecate in the street)

ALL YOU NEED IS:

Infant suppositories

Liverwurst cut in tiny pieces and wrapped in foil or plastic

The dog

Go out at the usual time. Insert the infant suppository completely
into the dog's rectum. Take him into the street and wait until he
defecates. Then praise him and give him a piece of liverwurst. Repeat
this procedure at normal walk (defecating) times for a few days. Then
begin taking him into the street without any suppository. Be sure to
praise him and give him the liverwurst when he defecates in the street!

If you give your dog the suppository and he does not defecate within
15 minutes, give him another--or as many as necessary to make him
defecate. If he is a large dog, you may wish to use adult size suppositories. Never return home without his defecating if he has been given
a suppository!

When you enter the street with your dog, try to use the middle of the
street as much as possible so that the stool is broken down quickly
by cars or street-cleaning equipment. Avoid crosswalks and building
entrance areas. And never, never permit your dog to defecate in the
parks or around trees and other plants.

If your dog is not fully under control yet (in housebreaking terms) or
if he has diarrhea, take a piece of cardboard or papertoweling with you
on your walks so you can clean up after him if he fouls the sidewalk.

Index

About the Author

PATRICIA P. WIDMER runs a dog-training service in New York City and lectures nationwide on dog-owner responsibility. Prominent in dog-welfare activities, she is a popular guest with TV emcees and nearly always brings along one or more dogs to demonstrate what she teaches.

Other SIGNET Books You'll Enjoy

More MENTOR and SIGNET Reference Books

(0451)

- [ ] **ALL ABOUT WORDS by Maxwell Numberg and Morris Rosenblum.** Two language experts call on history, folklore, and anecdotes to explain the origin, development, and meaning of words. (620712—$3.50)

- [ ] **HOW DOES IT WORK? by Richard Koff.** A practical and entertaining guide to the workings of everyday things—from air conditioners to zippers. Illustrated. (06920X—$1.50)

- [ ] **BEGIN CHESS by D. B. Pritchard.** An introduction to the game and to the basics of tactics and strategy. Foreword by Samuel Reshevesky, International Grand Master and former American chess champion. (115902—$1.75)

- [ ] **WORDS OF SCIENCE and the History Behind Them by Isaac Asimov.** A famous author makes the language of science accessible to all. Some 1500 terms are traced through history, from their simple roots in the language of bygone times—to their complicated usages today. (617991—$1.95)

- [ ] **WORDS FROM THE MYTHS by Isaac Asimov.** A fascinating exploration of our living heritage from the ancient world. Isaac Asimov retells the ancient stories—from Chaos to the siege of Troy—and describes their influence on modern language . . . and modern life. (113268—$1.75)
